CHANGING
WORL

CHANGING *the* WORLD

The Timeliness of Opus Dei

Martin Rhonheimer

 Scepter

CONTENTS

FOREWORD

The essays assembled in this volume are the fruit of personal reflection about a reality with which the author has been personally acquainted for more than thirty years. Indeed it is part of his life and identity. But although he has been a member of Opus Dei for quite sometime—first as a layman and since 1983 as a priest—the spirit and pastoral mission of this institution of the Catholic Church still make intellectual demands on him, as should be clear from these essays.

As the fruit of personal argumentation, the essays offer points of departure for a theological, philosophical, and historical presentation and analysis of what still is, after all, a novel and sometimes misunderstood spiritual and pastoral phenomenon. At the heart of these pages one will not find the institutional or organizational aspects of Opus Dei, but its specific spiritual and pastoral contours.

The essays do not pretend to be a learned or academic treatise, even though some do point to rather complex theological and historical implications. The author hopes he has succeeded in expressing himself in a generally understandable way. For details and further research the reader can consult the bibliographical material cited.

To some extent the subjects of the essays overlap. The second, until now unpublished, "Affirming the World and Christian Holiness," complements the first. This latter appeared in 2002 under the title "Blessed Josemaría and love for the world." It was part of a commemorative publication edited by Msgr. César Ortiz entitled *Josemaría Escrivá—Profile einer Gründergestalt* published by Adamas Verlag on the hundredth anniversary of the birth of the founder of Opus Dei.

The fourth essay, "Truth and Politics in Christian Society," offers a deeper continuation of the third essay, "The New Evangelization and Political Culture." It seeks to situate Opus Dei in the history of the Christian understanding of freedom as related to the reality of modern society and political pluralism. The texts of the essays have, where necessary, been updated and linked to one another editorially.

Changing the World is basically concerned with the ideal of Christian holiness in the midst of the world. For it is in the context of ordinary life's greatness and value, seen in the light of faith and the grace of divine filiation, that a frequently overlooked insight—namely, that the Church and the work of salvation carried out through her are for the deliverance and renewal of creation in Jesus Christ—finally is grasped and realized where people live and work.

Opus Dei is not a community or a group within the Church intended to gather together people who think alike in a refuge for pious contemplation, a hothouse isolated from the bustle of this world. It sees itself rather as an instrument of service to individual dioceses and a harmonious supplement to normal pastoral care—a pastoral instrument of the universal Church.

As a personal prelature, Opus Dei is a part of the Church's hierarchical structure. Its purpose is to recall what had almost been forgotten in the course of centuries: All of the faithful, wherever they live and work, are called on the basis of their baptism to the fullness of life in Christ, to holiness and apostolate, and therefore to full responsibility for the one single mission of the Church.

The formational program of the Prelature of Opus Dei is adapted according to the specific needs of individuals and never excludes anyone on social, ethnic, political, or religious grounds. Its founder, Josemaría Escrivá, who was canonized in 2002, called it—the "great catechesis." It is directed to the ordinary citizens of the world, to women and men of every social class, profession, and age—in order to help them understand, their lives and everyday occupations: as part of their Christian vocation, that includes jobs, marriages, families, studies, social and political activities, leisure time, and whatever else they do. It helps them as true contemplative souls to see these earthly realities not as hindrances, but, on the contrary, as paths to unity with God and fulfillment in the spirit of Christ.

In this way, they and their ordinary life become truly Church. The paths of the world are transformed into paths of God and, without losing their secularity and legitimate autonomy, become channels for proclamation of the faith and a true lay care of souls. Here is an apostolate present in all the pathways of human society, carried on by people who, like the early Christians, have no other ecclesiastical mission than the one they received in being baptized and so becoming Christ's. On this basis they know themselves called to be, in the words of St. Augustine, *alter Christus*, "another Christ," and as St. Josemaría Escrivá added, even *ipse Christus*, "Christ himself."

This specific spiritual and pastoral charism of Opus Dei not only expresses a central concern of the Second Vatican Council, but preceded it by several decades (Opus Dei began in 1928). The four essays included in this book seek to present it from different points of view and with different emphases.

The author hopes to make a small contribution to a deeper understanding of something that is in many respects a thoroughly new and, just for that reason, sometimes even grotesquely misunderstood phenomenon within the Church. To be sure, members of Opus Dei know themselves to be fallible men and women. St. Josemaría called himself "a sinner who is madly in love with Jesus Christ." But this consciousness of personal inadequacy does not excuse one from the responsibility of trying, with God's help and grace, to carry forward the spirit and charism of Opus Dei and make it fruitful for the Church and the world.

The book is dedicated to the memory of the Servant of God Pope John Paul II, of recent memory, by whom the author had the privilege of being ordained as a priest in 1983 in Rome, and who, among other things, helped to advance Opus Dei's apostolic work by establishing Opus Dei as a Personal Prelature in 1982 and by beatifying its founder in 1992 and canonizing him in 2002.

CHAPTER 1

Josemaría Escrivá and Love for the World

THE TWOFOLD NATURE OF THE WORLD

CHRISTIAN PASSION FOR THE WORLD

On an October day in the year 1967, in the midst of the campus of the University of Navarra, still under construction, before the façade of the library building and surrounded by bulldozers and cranes, the founder of Opus Dei, Josemaría Escrivá, celebrated the Eucharist surrounded by professors, students, and administrative personnel of the university. The university had been founded at his initiative, and was directed by members of Opus Dei. Today it counts some fifteen thousand students and faculty.

The homily given during this Mass was later published as *Passionately Loving the World*.[1] This title is a program that better than any other explains the nucleus of the spiritual message of Escrivá: Christian passion for the world, a passion nourished by faith in the God who created this world out of love in order to hand it over to the men and women whom he had created in his own image, to complete by their activity and labor the work that the Creator himself had said was

---

1. *Conversations with Josemaría Escrivá* (New York: Scepter Publishers, 2002): nos. 113–123.

"very good." It is a passion that springs from belief in that God who, after man turned away from his Creator and was unfaithful to his original vocation, became man himself in order to save man by giving us his own life and to appoint man as a collaborator in this work of salvation. In Christ and through his cleansing grace, the world can thereby return to its original goodness. The world is the real place and workplace of man and woman; it is their task, to which, in both the order of creation and the order of redemption, God has destined his beloved daughters and sons.

This optimistic message should not, however, be trivialized. "Passionate love for the world" can be misunderstood. It seems altogether in contradiction to a centuries-old tradition of spirituality and asceticism in which "the world" was looked upon rather as the enemy of mankind and as a hindrance to union with God, to holiness. But the very fact that St. Josemaría spoke of this passionate love for the world during the celebration of the Holy Eucharist may help us to avoid both banalization and any possible misunderstanding.

The Holy Eucharist is, of course, "the sacramental offering of the Body and Blood of the Lord," the sacrifice of our redemption, "the most sacred and transcendent act which man, with the grace of God, can carry out in this life. To communicate with the Body and Blood of our Lord is, in a certain sense, like loosening the bonds of earth and time, in order to be already with God in heaven, where Christ himself will wipe the tears from our eyes and where there will be no more death, nor mourning, nor cries of distress, because the old world will have passed away."[2]

"Love for the world" does not close its eyes to the world's transitory nature and need for renewal. With the eyes of Christ's love it looks at this world as in need of redemption. Yet it also knows it as that world which God at the moment of creation found to be "very good." Of course

---

2. Ibid., no. 113.

there is a perceptible tension here, a tension that is not only of a theological-theoretical kind, but, first of all, of a practical kind. This shows itself in the existential conflict of those who are aware of belonging very much to this world, who are as at home in it as fish in the sea, but who nevertheless experience the world as an adversary, a contradiction and hindrance to their nearness to God, even an occasion of sin, and through sin—through the evil and injustice of human hearts—deformed in so many ways that it often seems inconceivable that it could claim to be the work of a good, wise, and almighty Creator.

Yet it is precisely this aspect of the world as "adversary" and "hindrance" to a Christian life of unity with God and perfection in love—holiness—and of apostolate, that has long been at the center of the Christian ascetical and spiritual tradition (not least, through Western monastic-influenced spirituality). Today we are more conscious than formerly that this tradition was somewhat one-sided, a distortion as it were. From neither the spiritual nor the ascetical point of view can this vision of the world as hindrance to holiness and adversary to mankind be its decisive or fundamental aspect.

Indeed, in its one-sidedness it became an obstacle to the harmonious spiritual growth of the lay Christian, who in his normal role as an ordinary believer, in his ordinariness, became an extraordinary case: someone whom Christ had not really called to cooperate in his work of salvation. He or she was a second-class citizen of the Church, at best a collaborator of those who, having renounced the world to a greater or lesser degree and entered the tradition of *contemptus mundi* or at least become part of the clergy through a "vocation," had largely freed themselves from entanglement with the world so as at the same time to engage it from the outside. In this way, the structures of the world were used in the service of a greater spiritual-pastoral goal: to shield souls from worldly corruption and bring them to God: but not out of concern with the worldliness of these structures themselves and with their renewal in Christ, and so not really out of "love for the world."

THE WORLD: A WAY TO GOD

On this point Escrivá now raised his voice to proclaim a message that, as he often said, "was as old as the Gospel but at the same time as new as the Gospel." Holiness is not something for privileged persons, for a few within the great mass of believers who have received an additional or authentic call to the following of Christ. It is not intrinsically tied to renunciation of the world. God calls everyone through baptism to a life of holiness, to perfection of love, to an integral following of Christ, and to apostolate. The commissioning is received in baptism and confirmation. The Second Vatican Council made this universal call to holiness, which Josemaría Escrivá had been proclaiming since 1928, a substantial component of its message.[3]

But how often this teaching was misunderstood! It even led to a false superficial secularization of some who previously had said goodbye to the world but now were reintroduced to a changing world busy distancing itself from the Church, and who began to suffer from feelings of inferiority. They read the teaching of the Council as a demand to capitulate to the spirit of the age. And that was a misunderstanding. The Council did not mean to foster a laicizing or secularizing of members of religious orders and the clergy. It was not telling them to be modern and up to date and adapt themselves to the world. The Second Vatican Council in no way sought to open up new paths by which the clergy and religious could enter more freely into the world.

Nor did the Council intend some kind of "clericalization" of the laity, in the sense only of more lay involvement in the organizational structures of dioceses, parishes, and church

---

3. Cf. above all the Dogmatic Constitution on the Church *Lumen Gentium*, no. 39ff.

organizations. Rather, it proclaimed the Christian, sanctifying, co-redeeming value of the ordinary lives, lived in the middle of the world, of those Christians who up until then had been considered second-class in comparison with religious and clergy. As persons supposedly without vocations, "simple believers," they were seen exclusively as objects of pastoral care[4] (as if clerics and religious were not also believers and just as much, if not more, in need of spiritual care). The Second Vatican Council voiced an appeal for the rediscovery of just that great assemblage of believers who, practically speaking, had been forgotten when it came to Christian perfection and apostolic mission in the Church. Here was a rediscovery of baptism as the point of origin of the fundamental, definitive *vocation* and with it the rediscovery of ordinary Christian life and everyday existence in the midst of the world as a path of holiness and apostolate.[5]

This clearly calls for a new reflection on the relationship between Christian life and the world. "Passionate love for the world" therefore becomes with Josemaría Escrivá a program in contrast with the traditional program of *contemptus mundi*. This is not a criticism of the traditional renunciation of the world and the spirituality—"world disdaining" in an ascetical but not metaphysical sense—of the religious life. The founder of Opus Dei had a deep love for religious and their specific vocation, although he never felt personally called to it and knew it was not God's path for him. The spirituality of the religious orders continues to have its deep justification and its indelible meaning. It is the result of a divine charism in the Church, since "religious give outstanding and striking testimony that the world cannot be transfigured and offered to God without the spirit of the beatitudes."[6] Here is no depreciation of the spirituality of

4. Cf. *Lumen Gentium*, no. 30ff.

5. In this connection see various interviews in *Conversations with Josemaría Escrivá*, no. 20ff and no. 58ff.

6. *Lumen Gentium*, no. 31.

religious and their public, eschatological and conscience-stirring witness, but perhaps a new understanding of what is ordinary and what is not.

Since the Second Vatican Council, the ideas of holiness and Christian perfection can no longer be identified simply with a so-called state of perfection. The life of the laity, ordinary life in the world, can no longer be seen as involving a complete self-giving to God only in very extraordinary cases. And apostolate can no longer be viewed as a prerogative of the clergy and religious, with the laity considered only their co-workers. More often now it is just the reverse: the everyday life of the ordinary Christian in the midst of the world is regarded as a path to Christian perfection, not a hindrance and danger, while at the same time every Christian, thanks to baptism, has originally and directly received a mission to apostolate and apostolic responsibility within the Church. (This, to be sure, must always be carried on in communion with the shepherds appointed by Christ for his Church, the successor of the apostle Peter, the bishop of Rome, and the bishops in communion with him.)

Meanwhile, of course, "the world" must be understood somewhat differently in order not to contradict Christian tradition. The nexus is to be found in the idea of love for the world. To see it, in the light of sin, as the evil adversary of God and of man in his quest for loving relationships with his fellows, should no longer move one only to "contempt" for the world but to co-redeeming love, whose trajectory leads through the cross to the world's restoration, renewed in Christ, to God. This means that all created reality, even the least of it, the most ordinary and prosaic, has a lasting meaning. Taken up into this love, the created order plays a decisive role in the unfolding of the spiritual growth effected by the Spirit of God. This is a new kind of spirituality, one whose raw material is ordinary, everyday life and work in the middle of the world.

THE TWOFOLD CHARACTER OF THE WORLD

It was precisely on this point that St. Josemaría focused in his homily on the campus of the University of Navarra. The Mystery of the Eucharist, the sacrifice of Christ, points us to the new creation in Christ and thereby has a deeply eschatological meaning, reminding us of the transient nature of the present world. But this should not be misunderstood as meaning that for a Christian the things of this world have no real value, as if Christian life were "something exclusively 'spiritual,'" a life "proper to pure, extraordinary people, who remain aloof from the contemptible things of this world or, at most, tolerate them as something necessarily attached to the spirit, while we live on this earth."[7]

Were this the case, it would mean that "churches become the setting *par excellence* of the Christian life." Being a Christian would be equated with participation in sacred actions. The Christian's world would become a "segregated world, which is considered to be the ante-chamber of heaven, while the ordinary world follows its own separate path. The doctrine of Christianity and the life of grace would, in this case, brush past the turbulent march of human history, without ever really meeting it."[8] One has to say a "firm no" to "this deformed vision of Christianity." This is the "no" of the Christian who realizes that God is calling him to serve amid the ordinary realities of his life, especially in his professional work and his many family and social duties. For this daily life, as Escrivá explains to his hearers "is the true setting for your lives as Christians." "Where your fellow men, your yearnings, your work and your affections are, there you have your daily encounter with Christ."[9]

This certainty that one can encounter Christ just where someone with a "spiritualistic" mentality would least expect to find him rests on the clear awareness of the incarnation of

---

7. *Conversations*, no. 113.
8. Ibid.
9. Ibid.

God. In Jesus Christ, God became man and introduced the stuff of human life, especially the life of everyday, ordinary professional work, into the plan of redemption of the human race. "The fact that Jesus grew up and lived just like us shows us that human existence and all the ordinary activity of men have a divine meaning."[10] And even more, "after the Word of God has lived among the children of men, felt hunger and thirst, worked with his hands, experienced friendship and obedience and suffering and death," one can no longer claim "that there are things—good, noble, or indifferent—which are exclusively worldly."[11] Except only for the structures of sin, every earthly reality opens itself to the redeeming love of Christ and becomes—precisely as an earthly reality and according to its own logic—a path for this love, capable of being sanctified and saturated with the spirit of God.

This Christian optimism, rooted in faith, finally culminated in Josemaría Escrivá's often quoted exclamation, "The world is not evil, because it has come from God's hands, because it is His creation, because 'Yahweh looked upon it and saw that it was good' (cf. Gen 1:7ff). We ourselves, mankind, make it evil and ugly with our sins and infidelities."[12] This is a truly paradoxical formulation, for it says that the world is good and bad at the same time: good as God's work, but bad as the work of sin, which springs from the human heart. The formulation therefore appears to leave it undecided what attitude one should take towards this world—whether, as this real world in which we live, it is still good or whether, because of its deformation by sin, it has become a hindrance to a life of truly following Christ.

There is a solution if we keep in mind both sides of the paradox. "The world is good" is true, insofar as the world is

---

10. St. Josemaría, *Christ Is Passing By* (New York: Scepter, 1985): no. 14.
11. Ibid., no. 112.
12. *Conversations*, no. 114.

the work of God—and it always remains such, no matter how badly determined it is by men's sins. "The world is bad and ugly" also is true, insofar as we see the world only as the work of men and assuming this human work is not at the same time a work of God, *operatio Dei, opus Dei.* "The world is bad" is true only insofar as the human will is not united with the will of God, in this way striving for what is pleasing to God and so, with God's grace, overcoming sin and its consequences.

The original good of creation is in no way nullified by sin or made meaningless for Christian life: it is always there, though sometimes hidden and potential. Just as this original good was deformed, so it can be restored—and this through the same human will responsible for the evil in the world insofar as it joins itself to God. This is possible only through and in Christ: *per ipsum, et cum ipso, et in ipso,* as we say in the great doxology at the end of the Eucharistic prayer, "through him and with him and in him," or as St. Josemaría paraphrased it, "through my Love, with my Love, in my Love." In other words: "We must love the world, and work, and all human things. For the world is good. Adam's sin destroyed the divine balance of creation; but God the Father sent his only Son to re-establish peace, so that we, his children by adoption, might free creation from disorder and reconcile all things to God."[13]

This brings us to the heart of the question of human freedom. It stands at the crossroads where the destiny of this world is finally decided. Shall it become good, as God in his creative love wished it from all eternity, or shall it be a place far removed from God where the ruination of humankind takes place? "The Founder of Opus Dei is not addressing people who lead sheltered lives, but those who are fighting out in the open, in the most varied situations in life. In such circumstances, using their freedom, they come to the decision to serve God and love him above all things. Freedom is

---

13. *Christ Is Passing By,* no. 112.

something they cannot do without. Through it, their love grows firm and develops roots."[14]

MATERIALIZING THE SPIRITUAL LIFE

In the order of redemption it is precisely mankind's freedom that, moved by God's love, draws this world back to God. "Have no doubt: any kind of evasion of the honest realities of daily life is for you, men and women of the world, something opposed to the will of God."[15] Here St. Josemaría is thinking of work: the operating room in the university hospital, professorships and the classrooms, factories, workshops, the farmer's fields, offices of all kinds, conference rooms of large and small industries, the bustle of a shopping center, a household, family and neighborhood life. He is thinking, in short, of "all the immense panorama of work."[16] For there God "waits for us every day." It seems to be the realm only of secular, quotidian, material things, where people plug away at making a living or, perhaps, achieving their ambitions and expectations. It seems to be a place with no room for God. And yet the truth is that "there is something holy, something divine, hidden in the most ordinary situations, and it is up to each one of you to discover it."[17]

Discovering the *quid divinum*, the "divine something," in the "prose of each day" and making "heroic verse" of it[18] is the Christian's great task. As noted, it involves discovery precisely because at first glance there seems to be little of the holy or the divine in the prosaic reality of every day. To be sure, human beings seek the higher things, "the supernatural." Unless they have become resigned, they crave ecstasy and the

---

14. Alvaro del Portillo, Introduction to Josemaría Escrivá, *Friends of God* (New York: Scepter Publishers, 2002): p. 18.

15. *Conversations*, no. 114; cf. also *Christ Is Passing By*, no. 99.

16. *Conversations*, no. 114.

17. Ibid.

18. Ibid., no. 116.

great experience of fulfillment. In short, they want happiness. But people tend to identify this with breaking free of the ordinary and the everyday by means of extraordinary consolations and experiences. Up to a certain point, of course, that is understandable and even correct: we need festive occasions, a relief from everyday life, a relaxing and calming break in our routine. Yet, the greatest and most fulfilling experience actually comes in discovering that it is precisely in the ordinary and routine that one is most likely to have a true encounter with God. Perhaps it will be God on the cross, but even so it will be the God who created us from nothing and gives peace to our hearts, the happiness of "resting in him" which is just what we have always sought. "Our Lord had made me understand, and I tried to make other people understand, that the world is good, for the works of God are always perfect. . . . that we must love the world, because it is in the world that we meet God: God shows Himself, He reveals Himself to us in the happenings and events of the world."[19]

This is why St. Josemaría advised his listeners at the University of Navarra to learn "to 'materialize' their spiritual life." He warned them against a split personality of sorts, the temptation "of living a kind of double life. On one side, an interior life, a life of relation with God; and on the other, a separate and distinct professional, social and family life, full of small earthly realities."[20] We have only one heart for loving and only one life, "made of flesh and spirit. And it is that life which has to become, in both body and soul, holy and filled with God: we discover the invisible God in the most visible and material things."[21] Escrivá goes even further: he claims that for a Christian living in the world—the ordinary Christian—there is no other way to encounter God and to orient himself in relation to his life as it really is.

---

19. Ibid., no. 70.
20. Ibid., no. 114.
21. Ibid.

To be sure, the sacraments are decisive for enabling the life of grace to grow in us. They are what the "early Christians described as the footprints of the Incarnate Word," through which we each receive the "love of God, with all its creative and redemptive power."[22] But that is not sufficient of itself. Indeed, it is simply a means to the real end: the very personal response that God wants from each individual person in his specific situation, so that his life becomes cooperation in the work of redemption and unfolds as a way of personal holiness and apostolate. "There is no other way. Either we learn to find our Lord in ordinary, everyday life, or else we shall never find Him." Ordinary life, the world of work, family, recreation, and all that belongs to these things—in fact, all these "most trivial occurrences and situations"—must become "a means and an occasion for a continuous meeting with Jesus Christ."[23]

CO-REDEMPTIVE EFFECTIVENESS

We have here a truly "lay" spirituality. It is a spirituality not formed on the model of a state of perfection and then applied to the situation of the Christian in the world (to which it is in its origins not at all applicable) with the aim of squeezing the lives of lay people into a kind of spiritual corset. Rather, this is a spirituality which had its origin, as was said, precisely in the situation of the ordinary Christian, one whose material comes from a genuine secularity—a situation comprised of all those earthly relationships and tasks that make up a typical human life, which such a spirituality equips with supernatural wings rather than a spiritual corset.

These intuitive formulations rest on a very meaningful and, one might say, somewhat revolutionary theological view of the reality that since Vatican II has been called the general or universal call to holiness. For hundreds of years, people

---

22. Ibid., no. 115.
23. Ibid., no. 114.

thought of the universality of the vocation to holiness only in its subjective dimension: i.e., everyone personally, as a subject, is called to attain holiness. God, wrote St. Paul, "desires all men to be saved and to come to the knowledge of the truth" (1 Tim 2:4). No human being is excluded from this general salvific will of God. Every person without exception is capable of attaining holiness.

Rather different, however, is the objective dimension of this salvific will, namely, "that all the situations and circumstances of ordinary life can and should be the place and medium of communion with God, of sanctification. For the majority of Christians, immersed as they are in temporal activities and situations in the midst of the world, holiness is possible not in spite of —not even outside of—ordinary life: it is to be found precisely *in and through* the incidents of that ordinary life."[24]

The objective character of this general vocation to holiness also means (and this is new and in Opus Dei's early days led some influential Spanish churchmen close to the Roman Curia to claim that young Father Escrivá might be guilty of heresy) that there is in this world no privileged place for attaining Christian perfection, so that for this purpose one does not necessarily have to be in a state of perfection but need only seek sanctity in his or her own state, including the state of matrimony. Thus all earthly realities and human activities, insofar as they are not sinful *in themselves* and therefore contrary to the will of God, can be means or paths to unity with God, precisely because *in themselves* they are good as realities made and willed by God.[25]

---

24. Fernando Ocáriz, "Vocation to Opus Dei as a Vocation in the Church," in Pedro Rodríguez, Fernando Ocáriz, and José Luis Illanes, *Opus Dei in the Church: An Ecclesiological Study of the Life and Apostolate of Opus Dei* (Dublin: Four Courts; Princeton, NJ: Scepter, 1994): pp. 90–91.

25. In regard to the concept of Christian perfection: deliberately, the word perfection is not used here by itself, and we speak of "Christian perfection." The reason is that this is not perfection in the sense of being free of error or any other sort of flawlessness or purely human perfection. Christian perfection is the perfection of

This teaching, taken for granted by the Fathers of the Church such as St. Augustine and St. John Chrysostom and by the early Christians in general, had been almost entirely forgotten over the centuries, even though saints such as Francis de Sales and numerous spiritual authors repeatedly and more or less clearly reminded people of it. In practice, spiritual life for Christians living in the world, even when it was recommended, was thought to be something over and above ordinary life. Apostolate was at best cooperation with the apostolate of the hierarchy or the religious orders. That life in the world is, as such, a place and means of spiritual life, of prayer, of contemplation, of unity with God and an apostolate stemming from it carried on by one who is a genuine participant in the Church's mission, even apart from any Church structures—even today all this seems so new that in its terse, yet explosive simplicity it is still often not understood, perhaps because of that very simplicity.

Josemaría Escrivá always urged his spiritual daughters and sons to turn all of life into prayer. It is not work that is the "weapon" of Opus Dei, but prayer, and daily work must therefore be turned into prayer. For this to happen, of course, the work must first of all be good, competent work done in the service of one's fellow men and the whole of society. It is done out of love of God precisely inasmuch as it is turned into prayer and spiritual strength uniting mankind with God and giving a co-redeeming efficacy to one's entire life. "I assure you," Escrivá told his audience at the University of Navarra, "when a Christian carries out with love the most insignificant everyday action, that action overflows with the transcendence of God. . . . Heaven and earth

---

the children of God in their love for God their Father through the Holy Spirit. It is always the perfection of sinners and is fully compatible with human limitation and weakness. Christian perfection is not something elite or self-righteous; it expresses itself in humility and love, and in the noble effort to overcome one's mistakes and fulfill God's will in everything, according to the dictates of a conscience formed by the Church. This is the sort of union with God and holiness that people can—to varying degrees in each case—attain in this life.

seem to merge . . . on the horizon. But where they really meet is in your hearts, when you sanctify your everyday lives." [26]

Josemaría Escrivá here saw the redeeming and cleansing power of the Holy Spirit at work. He cited St. Paul—"all are yours; and you are Christ's; and Christ is God's" (1 Cor 3:22–23), and "whether you eat or drink, or whatever you do, do all to the glory of God" (1 Cor 10:31)—and called this "an ascending movement, which the Holy Spirit, infused in our hearts, wants to call forth from this world, upwards from the earth to the glory of the Lord. Everything is included, he insists, "even what seems most commonplace."[27]

This teaching of Holy Scripture, which belongs to the "very nucleus of the spirit of Opus Dei," leads the believing Catholic to "do your work perfectly, to love God and mankind by putting love in the little things of everyday life, and discovering that divine something which is hidden in small details."[28]

It is precisely at this point that "Christian materialism"[29] and optimism come into clear focus. "To do one's work as perfectly as possible" in order to serve one's fellowmen, to put love into even the small details of everyday life: surely that sounds almost too beautiful and too much of this world to suit the need. And yet it is right here that one comes to the true heart of the matter. We are not asked merely to be industrious and upright, never to harm anyone, to fulfill our duty and in all things seek the honor of God. It is a matter of seeking the greatest possible perfection in what one does in one's profession, family, education, free time, social relationships and so on, striving to live the spirit of Christ without compromise: a spirit of service, of self-giving, of forgiveness, of inner detachment from the goods of the world, of obedience to the will of God,

---

26. *Conversations*, no. 116.

27. Ibid., no. 115.

28. Ibid., no. 116.

29. Ibid., no. 116.

of giving one's own life, "even to death on the cross." In most cases this means self-denial, putting oneself in the background, seeking the honor of God with an upright intention. All the traditional themes of Christian asceticism appear here.

What it really comes down to is continuing the original creation covenant, though now with the strengthening of Christ's redemptive love, for the love of God and—in and through this love—for love of one's fellow man (not for selfish motives, careerism, one's own satisfaction or recognition, etc.). This means working to make this world a place where God dwells and justice and peace reign. That includes reconciling faith and culture with one another and seeking to bring an end to the disastrous separation and frequent antagonism between scientific-technical advances, culture, and modern civilization on the one side and Christian faith and the Church on the other, and to foster a fruitful collaboration and unity between them.

To be sure, it is just here that problems and contradictions could arise. It might be suspected that what was envisaged was a new and dangerous integralism.[30] One must also bear in mind that those to whom this message is directed—and indeed those who proclaim it—are sinners. These too are "children of Eve" and in need of redemption. "Love for the world" is all well and good, but it can also be a perverse love. It is precisely as one attempts to realize so fine-sounding a program that the world may show itself as opponent, as hindrance, as great temptress. The outcome of loving the world might then be turning away from God and becoming entangled in the sin and downfall of mankind.

REBELS FOR LOVE

By no means is the traditional and often rather one-sided view of the world as hindrance and temptation altogether unjustified.

---

30. We will not take up this matter here. In regard to it see chapter 3 entitled "The New Evangelization and Political Culture."

Now, however, in the light of what we have been saying it appears in quite a new way. We are not being warned to renounce this world nor is judgment being passed upon it by asserting that one can find God only by passing beyond the world (despite having to live in it) while at the same time having to dodge and neutralize its seductive appeal through spiritual exercises. "The world" now much more resembles a mission and a program, an entity that must be sanctified from within, albeit by a process that begins with oneself. For each of us is part of this world and is his or her own first and greatest hindrance on the path to God.

Passionate love for the world must not overlook something that the apostle and evangelist St. John brings sharply into focus: insofar as it is filled with evil, this world is characterized by "the lust of the flesh and the lust of the eyes and the pride of life" (1 Jn 2:16). Here are covetousness of every kind, pride, and arrogance, moving the beloved apostle of our Lord to warn: "Do not love the world or the things in the world. If anyone loves the world, love for the Father is not in him" (1 Jn 2:15).

St. Josemaría grasped this Johannine teaching that the world is a danger in a realistic manner,[31] but at the same time he evaluated it properly. It is not the world as such—God's creation and the natural human habitat—that is man's enemy, but the "world" of which John speaks: a disordered state of mind and spirit, above all pride, self-conceit, vanity, disordered self-love, and all the vices that spring from these things. The world in this sense is the corrupted heart of mankind, which became enmeshed in worldly goods—yes, even through their beauty and inner perfection—and set them in the Creator's place. The world in this sense is the Augustinian *civitas terrena*, the earthly city, here-and-now reality infused with disordered self-love to the extent that one feels contempt for God. This too-worldly world is set against the *civitas Dei*,

---

31. Cf. *Christ Is Passing By*, no. 4.

the city of God, where one loves God to the extent of contempt for self.

Here we see the real "sin of the world," which St. Paul identified with the sin of the "pagans." "They exchanged the truth about God for a lie and worshipped and served the creature rather than the Creator. . . . They were filled with all manner of wickedness, evil, covetousness, malice. Full of envy, murder, strife, deceit, malignity, they are gossips, slanderers, haters of God, insolent, haughty, boastful, inventors of evil, disobedient to parents, foolish faithless, heartless, ruthless" (Rom 1:25, 29–31). This is a picture of the world as we see it today wherever Christ's spirit does not rule, as is often the case among Christians themselves, even within the Church, in its very structures.

But such an analysis does not necessarily lead to withdrawal from the world nor to the judgment that worldly realities are in themselves a hindrance to true love of God. Josemaría Escrivá had painted on a frieze in Villa Tevere, the central headquarters of Opus Dei in Rome, these words of our Lord's prayer for his disciples: "I do not pray that thou shouldst take them out of the world, but that thou shouldst keep them from the evil one" (Jn 17:15). The point is that the Christian, as a child of God, is called, with the help of the grace that Christ asked from the Father, to cleanse the world of sin and restore to all these earthly realities their original goodness: to order them according to the will of God and thereby "to put the Cross of Christ on the summit of all human activities," as Josemaría Escrivá would say.

Here, however, one must not think of a political program. This is the overcoming of the structures of sin in the hearts of men and women, and thereby also in society, in human interrelationships and arrangements of all kinds. "Sanctification of work," carrying out work with the "greatest possible perfection," now is seen as a task and a mission that goes far beyond any righteous fulfillment of duty. It is much more a question of restructuring the world in Christ, through the love of

Christ, in the power of the Holy Spirit. And it is precisely this that constitutes a spirituality tailor-made for the average Christian in the world—although, strictly speaking, not really "tailor-made" since it is based on the secularity of the ordinary Christian, on his pre-existing, natural situation, which only needs to be discovered with the help of faith. "There is something holy, something divine, hidden in the most ordinary situations, and it is up to each one of you to discover it." St. Paul's catalog of the vices of the pagans, cited above, shows us the direction. What is asked of us is an inner struggle, a battle against oneself, to live all of the virtues: the human virtues—justice, wisdom, courage, temperance, and with them patience, detachment (poverty), chastity, serenity, industriousness, cheerfulness, tolerance, and so many others; and the theological virtues given by God to man—faith, hope, and charity.[32]

Christian life is not simply summed up in what are traditionally called the evangelical counsels. These are at once too few and too many. Too few, since not only poverty, chastity, and obedience, but all of the virtues are required. And too many, because the spirituality of the evangelical counsels is tied to the idea of a state of perfection occupied by those who, dedicating themselves to God and the Church, conform their lives to the counsels. In doing so, they separate themselves from ordinary life as members of religious communities and are also essentially separated from worldly cares.

This is not the way for the ordinary Christian. He needs no other state than the one he already occupies as a citizen of this world. And he needs no other consecration than that received in baptism and confirmation. For these carry a vocation "to put on Christ," to be another Christ, to be Christ himself, which also means living the human and theological

---

32. See Josemaría Escrivá, *Friends of God*. Also, since Christian morality is a morality of virtues, see also Martin Rhonheimer, *Die Perspektive der Moral: Philosophische Grundlagen der Tugendethik* (Berlin: 2001), Epilogue. (Forthcoming in English as *The Perspective of Morality*, Catholic University of America Press, Washington D.C.)

virtues in accord with one's gifts and allowing oneself to be led by the spirit of God.

The virtues are a sufficient answer to the various dangers that arise from the world (in the Johannine sense). Yet even today many people still view these dangers as virtually insurmountable hindrances to a consistent Christian life. Modern life itself seems to have so many functional constraints and structures of sin, which place great pressure on the individual, that prospects of living a halfway upright and honest life can seem nil.

Think of people involved in finance or banking, managers of international companies, physicians, hospital personnel, genetic researchers, teachers at all levels, journalists who have to speed up the filing of their stories to help their news organizations stay financially afloat. Think, too, of parents, who as they labor to raise their children often run into apparently insurmountable obstacles and misunderstandings, so that bringing children into the world and raising them correctly can come to seem almost unbearably difficult. Think of the agitated and irregular rhythm of life today that often leaves no time for rest and leisure—the schedules of airline pilots, shift workers, or those involved in hotel work, for instance—and then consider the many thousands who are prisoners of a daily routine and have nothing to look forward to except holidays, weekends, vacations, and finally retirement in secure prosperity. Reflect on the sea of sense-stimuli that flood people's eyes and ears and the outpourings of the entertainment industry (in which nevertheless Christians should be able to be active—something highly desirable, in fact).

In the face of all this one may reasonably ask, how is anyone supposed to live a life of radical following of Christ, a life of holiness, of unity with God and apostolic efficacy? How, in all of those areas, can one present work that is "perfect" and "pleasing to God" as an offering? Aren't people plagued by very different concerns—for financial security, for health, for success and career advancement—along with preoccupations centered on consuming, enjoying the beautiful and pleasant in art, sports, nature, vacations, etc.?

Indeed, while ordinary life does contain stimuli, problems, and perspectives, it also often brings with it dullness and apathy, the oppressive presence of evil and temptation—or at least of distraction, mediocrity, and simply going with the tide—and finally an emotional deadness.

But this is a faulty picture that requires correcting. Who says financial services, banking, and asset management are bad things in themselves? Why should the work of journalists and physicians, despite their problems, be impediments to helping one's fellow man and loving God? And as for the tension of the pilot and the weariness of the shift-worker, the efforts of politicians to win elections and have their bills enacted, the joys and sorrows of parents with their children and their family worries, with all the thousand little things they entail—aren't all these opportunities to give oneself in service of others, to pour out one's life doing good, and so to love and give glory to God? Yes, even the people involved in the entertainment industry—artists, actors, musicians—are all performing meaningful service on behalf of their fellowmen, which possesses unsuspected possibilities of apostolic efficacy!

Are wishing for a successful career, a higher income, health, the joyful experience of art, sports, and nature forms of turning away from God and opposed to a life that unfolds in apostolic effectiveness, or are they not instead just different ways of showing oneself thankful for the gifts of God and of using one's talents? Is Christ really foreign to all of these realities? Here is the very heart of it: to learn that we must find him—the demands of his love and also his cross—precisely in these realities.

Often, of course, living virtuously in a working context means having to forgo a promotion or a raise. It may even mean brutal misunderstanding and rejection, loss of a job, social scorn. But even so, why should wanting a career, success, and profit be considered bad in itself? All of this can be good when it is not in conflict with loving God, serving one's fellow men, and developing greater apostolic effectiveness. This does not mean reducing the innate goodness of earthly realities to a mere means or tool for achieving spiritual aims. Someone like Josemaría Escrivá, who could say that seeing the Capitoline Venus could move him to thank God for making human beings so beautiful and that for him the marriage bed was comparable to an altar, would not make that mistake.[33] Worldly things are not to be reduced to "mere means." They are to be elevated to their final and highest purpose: to manifest God's creative love and splendor.

This naturally requires an inner struggle, a constant battle against oneself for love of God.[34] "Good and evil are mixed in human history, and therefore the Christian should be a man of judgment. But this judgment should never bring him to deny the goodness of God's works. On the contrary, it should bring him to recognize the hand of God working through all human actions, even those which betray our fallen nature."[35] The virtues—the spiritual struggle to acquire them and to foster their growth—are the key to a consistent Christian life lived in the midst of the world, with its renewal in view. "Christ's invitation to sanctity, which he addresses to all men without exception, puts each one of us under an obligation to cultivate our interior life and to struggle daily to practice the Christian virtues; and not just in any way whatsoever, nor in a way which is above average or even excellent. No; we must strive to the point of heroism, in the strictest and most exacting sense of the word."[36] That, as Josemaría stressed, demands self-denial and a robust "interior mortification,"

---

33. Josemaría Escrivá made this remark in the presence of an audience of several thousand people in Buenos Aires during one of his catechetical trips in 1974.

34. See, for example, *Christ Is Passing By*, no. 73 ff.

35. *Conversations*, no. 70.

36. *Friends of God*, no. 3.

constant purification of intention, and then, again and again, a resolute "no" to the temptations of the world. Only a true, deep, and genuine inner life, constant contact with God in his threefold personhood as Father, Son, and Holy Spirit—the life that comes from prayer and from the grace of God given to us through the sacraments of the Church—can give the strength to identify oneself with Christ in ordinary life, to become "another Christ," "Christ himself."[37]

Everyday heroism is more than mere "being good." "Today it is not enough for men and women to be good. Moreover, whoever is content to be nearly . . . good, is not good enough. It is necessary to be 'revolutionary.' Faced by hedonism, faced by the pagan and materialistic wares that we are being offered, Christ wants objectors!—rebels of Love!"[38]

Thus, precisely out of love for this world, passionate love for the world becomes rebellion. It is not expressed in grand gestures but in the daily grind that, with its thousand demands for self-giving in the service of one's fellow men, can be seen as that which is truly great and meaningful. Only the interior life, association with God in prayer and the sacraments, can reveal the true greatness of the everyday. "Rest assured that you will usually find few opportunities for dazzling deeds, one reason being that they seldom occur. On the other hand, you will not lack opportunities, in the small and ordinary things around you, of showing your love for Christ."[39]

Trivial as this may sound, as a living reality it is far from trivial. In the same vein is Josemaría Escrivá's warning against what he called *mística ojalatera* ("tin-can mysticism"). In Spanish, this is a play on words that refers back to the expression *ojalá* ("if only"): "if only I had stayed single," "if only I were in a different profession," "if only I had better health, if

---

37. Cf. *Christ Is Passing By*, no. 104.

38. Josemaría Escrivá, *Furrow*, no. 128.

39. *Friends of God*, no. 8.

only I were still young, if only I were a little older." [40] And the catalog of these "if onlys" goes on endlessly: "if only my husband didn't have this tick," "If only my wife . . . my employer . . . my fellow worker . . . the atmosphere . . . the society . . . my neighbor . . . "

Tin-can mysticism is a flight from reality, and for Christians it is mainly a flight from the cross as well—a way of insulating oneself against having to recognize that precisely in *this* situation, with *these* people, with their peculiarities and failings, the response of love and self-giving is demanded and is the way of peace, of Christian joy, of apostolic fruitfulness. "Leave behind false idealism, fantasies, and what I usually call mystical wishful thinking. . . . Instead turn seriously to the most material and immediate reality, which is where our Lord is."[41] That is a powerful statement—"which is where our Lord is"—and it means: Just there is where this *quid divinum* is to be discovered, just there is this "holy and divine," there is the fulcrum for the lever by which the grace of God, through our cooperation, can change the world. To turn seriously to the most material and immediate reality does not mean simply accepting the status quo and putting up with everything. Instead it signifies the "rebellion of love"—responding with love to everything, for "by this all men will know that you are my disciples, if you have love for one another" (Jn 13:35).

CONTEMPLATIVES IN THE MIDST OF THE WORLD

The head of a large and well-known Catholic publishing house once asked me what I regarded as the most urgent concern for the Church in our time. Without thinking about it, I spontaneously said that it probably was that people finally understand the task of the lay Christian in the world, the real

---

40. *Conversations*, no. 116.
41. Ibid.

mission of the lay person in the Church. Taken aback, my questioner said that surely these were two quite *different* matters. I replied that precisely this—the habit of considering these to be two different subjects—showed how urgent the problem was. Let me spell out what I mean.

The mission of the Church is to fill the world with the spirit of Christ. "Passionate love of the world," as proclaimed by Josemaría Escrivá—unity of worldly existence and spiritual life, sanctification of the everyday and of ordinary work, the common priesthood of the faithful—is a fulfillment in the highest degree of the original mission of the Church. To live as Christians in the middle of the world and lead the world back to God is the true *ecclesial* mission of the lay person. Indeed, it is in a certain sense the mission of the Church itself, realized only in this "becoming Christ" of the laity (or better, the ordinary Christian). Everything else, the administrative bodies of the Church and work in ecclesiastical structures, exists only to serve this as means to a goal; only in rare, exceptional cases is it the place for lay people to fulfill what it means for them to be Christ and the Church.

The problem lies in how the word "Church" is understood. It is "frequently used in a clerical sense as meaning 'proper to the clergy or the Church hierarchy'"—proper, that is, to ecclesiastical structures. "And therefore many people understand participation in the life of the Church simply, or at least principally, as helping in the parish, cooperating in associations that have a mandate from the hierarchy, taking an active part in the liturgy, and so on. Such people forget in practice, though they may agree in theory, that the Church comprises all the People of God. All Christians go to make up the Church. Therefore *the Church is present wherever there is a Christian who strives to live in the name of Christ.*"[42]

In such an ecclesiological perspective, "passionately loving the world" would simply be a participation in the redeeming

---

42. Ibid., no. 112, italics added.

love of Christ, the co-redeeming love of Christians, in the actual carrying-out of the real mission of Christ's Church. Insofar as the Christian living in the world is Christ himself, he is also the Church. Of course, as has been said, this does not refer to an activist program. For more it is simply a matter of ordinary life in the middle of this world and its structures, life as it is lived by thousands and millions of men and women who, like the early Christians, in deep union with our Lord act in their own environment as leaven in the mass and seek to serve as light and "the salt of the earth."[43]

In his biography of the founder of Opus Dei, Peter Berglar recalls how during the Vatican Council a bishop spoke to St. Josemaría Escrivá about its being the laity's role "to fill the world with Christian life and transform the structures of the temporal order." He answered: "Yes, Your Excellency, but only if they have a contemplative soul. Otherwise they will not transform anything at all; rather they will be the ones transformed."[44]

The "love for the world" must be the love of Christ, and it is possible only when the Christian placed in the middle of this world is a contemplative who therefore lives as a child of his heavenly Father and in union with Christ on the cross. Precisely that is the essential insight underlying this sentence spoken on the campus of the University of Navarra: "There is something holy, something divine, hidden in the most ordinary situations, and it is up to each one of you to discover it."[45] To repeat: usually this does not mean doing anything out of the ordinary. Great Christian love is realized in the often small and inconspicuous duties of everyday life. "You can climb to the top of your profession, you can gain the highest acclaim as a reward for your freely chosen endeavors in

---

43. Cf. ibid., no. 24.

44. Peter Berglar, *Opus Dei: Life and Work of its Founder, Josemaría Escrivá* (Princeton: Scepter, 1984/1994): p. 248.

45. *Conversations*, no. 114.

temporal affairs; but if you abandon the supernatural outlook that should inspire all our human activities, you will have gone sadly astray."[46]

In everyday life, with its successes and failures, its frequent monotony, but also the glitter and high points of a professional career with all its legitimate human expectations and disappointments, in the midst of joy and sorrow, discovering the greatness of God and the fullness of Christ's love changes and renews this world, so that it is possible to say of creation that "God saw it and it was good."[47]

What is required therefore is a deep "unity of life" in which the divine and the human blend, linked to a true "lay mentality"[48] that is characterized among other things by accepting responsibility for oneself, respecting the opinions

---

46. *Friends of God*, no. 10.

47. It seems useful at this point to note that the Reformation brought a rediscovery of the common priesthood (to be sure, at the price of the devaluation and misunderstanding of ordained priesthood), and with it a substantial correction to what—on quite understandable historical grounds—had become the very clerical and monastically formed spiritual world of the Middle Ages (wherein, to be sure, the monastic idea had in turn been distorted and misunderstood). Above all, within English and Anglo-American Calvinism or Puritanism (somewhat less in Lutheranism) there took place in this perspective, an upgrading of "ordinary life" and its sanctification. The world was viewed as a place of mission for men (only those who were justified by faith). Earthly activities are good in themselves, but have become a source of sin through the perversion of hearts. They can and must become a means to love God [see in this regard Charles Taylor, *Sources of the Self: The Making of the Modern Identity*, (Cambridge, 1989, especially Part III "The Affirmation of Ordinary Life")]. Here we cannot consider how far the Protestant-Puritan perspective diverges from the Catholic view of co-redemption and *consecratio mundi* and falls into a duality of "inner-worldly asceticism" (Max Weber) on the one side and a "use of the world for the glory of God" on the other, and so seems to fall short precisely in respect to "passionate love for the world" and what is linked to it, and even anchored in it, i.e., Christian perfection. (For this, see chapter 2, "Affirming the World and Christian Holiness.") We must not forget, however, that Calvinism was not only interested in guarding the faithful from the temptations of the world, but also understood it to be their mission to re-order earthly conditions. Just there does its modernity lie. The significance of St. Josemaría concerns precisely the fact that he brings together this modern theme of renewing earthly realities and biblical redemption theology—the ideal of Christian perfection and its ascetical-mystical tradition, as well as the humanistic motive of love for the world—and thereby opens up in a completely new way the prospect of reconciling Christian tradition and the modern.

48. *Conversations*, no. 117.

of others, their legitimate differences and pluralism, and not using the Church for personal, purely human interests. A lay mentality is demanded by genuine Christian secularity and so by real Christian love for the world, which is nothing other than Christ's love for it. Lay mentality and Christian secularity do not propose to abolish the worldliness of the world, but to saturate it with the love of Christ and thereby direct it to its true goal.

OASES OF SPIRITUAL AND APOSTOLIC IMPETUS

The founder of Opus Dei did not just preach about these things. God called him to be an instrument for the founding of Opus Dei, which has been established by the Holy See as the Prelature of the Holy Cross and Opus Dei. This pastoral institution of the universal Church has as its goal the universal dissemination of this universal call to holiness directed to Christians—the fact that life in the midst of the world is a divine path, a path to God.

As a pastoral structure of the universal Church in the service of the local churches, Opus Dei enables Christians to discover the sanctifying value of ordinary work. It does this through its members who, like the early Christians live in all strata of society and are called above of all to make this spirit their own, and also through its many centers and corporate works scattered throughout the world. These oases of spiritual renewal, spiritual formation, and apostolic impetus offer people concrete help in living the spirit of contemplation and apostolate in the midst of everyday life, discovering the sanctifying value of ordinary work, and especially becoming conscious of the Christian consequences and demands of their vocation.

This is doubtless an enrichment of the Church that supplements the normal care of souls available in parishes. It goes far beyond what the parish can do because it nurtures apostolate and a presence of the Church in society—a way of being "at home" in the workplace, the neighborhood, the family that pastoral efforts ordinarily cannot reach. One can see here no less than a mobilization of the mass of ordinary Christians for the Kingdom of God. The first requirement, on which everything else depends, is that Catholics be conscious of being called, of having a vocation, to renew this world in Christ through their co-redeeming love for it.

First of all it is a question of faith. And that is how the homily preached at that Mass on the campus of the University of Navarra concluded: "Faith is a virtue which we Christians need greatly. . . . For without faith, we lack the very foundation for the sanctification of everyday life."[49] Only with the eyes of faith can everyday, ordinary human life in this world be seen as a supernatural adventure, an opportunity to renew everything in Christ, so that God be all in all.

---

49. *Conversations*, no. 123.

CHAPTER 2

Affirming the World and Christian Holiness

JOSEMARÍA ESCRIVÁ'S REDISCOVERY OF ORDINARY LIFE

THE GENERAL CALL TO HOLINESS AND "PASSIONATE LOVE FOR THE WORLD"

In the neighborhood of the village of Pereto on the edge of the Abruzzi region of Italy, not far from Rome, is a pilgrimage site where our Lady is honored under the title of *Madonna dei Bisognosi*, Our Lady of the Needy. The restored shrine church contains a large fresco of the Last Judgment painted by a local artist at the end of the fifteenth century. This grandiose work of art speaks very clearly. On one side lies paradise: it is inhabited exclusively by priests, nuns, and other members of religious orders. In purgatory, on the other hand, the astonished viewer sees representatives of all the professions of that day, ordinary Christians of every kind.[1]

That painting expresses something taken for granted for centuries: although God certainly wants everyone to go to heaven and be holy in the sight of God, only those who renounce life in the world and enter the state of perfection as religious or at least become priests can hope to live lives

---

1. For this item I am indebted to Giorgio Faro; cf. Giorgio Faro, *Il lavoro nell'insegnamento del beato Josemaría Escrivá* (Rome: 2000): p. 92.

completely pleasing to God and achieve perfection in loving God. He who lives in the world unavoidably dirties his hands—that is, his soul—and if he is not lost forever, at least needs purification after this life.

The message is clear: the ideal of Christian life and Christian perfection is renunciation of the world. Following Christ in a consistent and radical way is possible only by renouncing ordinary, earthly life. This theological perspective was in no way shared by the early Christians, but it was spelled out clearly, in the course of the Middle Ages, and later was questioned by a very few (for example St. Francis de Sales).

Given this background, it is perhaps understandable why in 1928 the young Josemaría Escrivá encountered mistrust, rejection, and misunderstanding from more than a few of his contemporaries. For he maintained that all Christians without exception were called to holiness, to the fullness of Christian life, to intimate friendship with God, and to identification with Christ, and that they were called in the midst of ordinary life, in the hectic activity of one's job and everyday cares, in the intimacy of married life, in family life, among social engagements, politics, and business. One can find God everywhere, even in daily work and the apparent monotony and sameness of the ordinary. It is not just a few privileged persons who are meant to strive effectively and with apostolic fruitfulness for holiness. The great Christian goal of love of God and thereby of all mankind is, according to Escrivá, accessible to all. Life in the midst of the world is not a hindrance. On the contrary, just that ordinary everyday work can be a path to God. In short, not just priests and members of religious orders have a "vocation" and full responsibility for the mission of the Church. All people, without exception, do.

Baptism itself brings with it a "vocation," God's call and his choice. "You, therefore, must be perfect, as your heavenly Father is perfect."[2] Christ proclaimed that to all who heard

---

2. Mt 5:48.

his Sermon on the Mount: women and men, grown-ups and children, the healthy and sick, single and married, manual workers, farmers, fishers, tax collectors, businessmen, intellectuals.[3] To be baptized means that one has received from God, always and only in union with Christ, the mission of sanctifying the world from within it, bringing the work of redemption to completion, and through the sanctification of ordinary life and the permeation of all earthly realities with the spirit of Christ reconciling creation with God.

Why then should ordinary Catholics—married couples, people who spend their whole lives in professional work and caring for their families, raising children, cooperating in the progress of science and technology, and contributing as Christians to peace and justice in society—have less need to strive for perfection in love? Did not Christ himself, the Word of God made man, spend the greater part of his life working in a carpentry shop in a tiny village in Galilee? Why should living in this world and doing human work be, not a path to God but, by its very essence a hindrance to unity with God and perfect identification with Christ and his mission?

Yet this was in fact a widely held view, theologically cemented—although never proclaimed as such by the magisterium of the Church—that became almost normative in pastoral practice. If someone had a "vocation," he or she was no longer an ordinary Christian, since ordinary folk did not have vocations. One could not even consider marriage as a truly Christian vocational path.

It was the God-given charism of St. Josemaría Escrivá to break free from this narrow view and remind us that in no way was this the perspective of the Gospel or of the early Christians and the Fathers of the Church. Thus St. Josemaría saw the central message of Opus Dei as something "as old as the Gospel, and like the Gospel still new." It was "old" in corresponding to the original spirit of Christ. It was "new"

---

3. Cf. Josemaría Escrivá, *The Way*, no. 291.

because in the course of centuries it had been almost completely forgotten.

The founder of Opus Dei was far from wishing to deni-
grate in any way the vocation of religious. On the contrary: he
loved the religious vocation with all his heart and saw in it a
special sign of God's love and an absolutely essential treasure
for the Church. At the same time, he admitted that he was
saddened when he entered a cloister. He told those for whom
he was spiritual director that they too should "passionately
love" the world, since it was God's work, coming from his
hand and therefore good. It became bad only through sin,
which comes from the heart of man through misuse of our
"freedom, a gift from God."[4] Each and every person who follows Christ's call has the task of rediscovering the face of God
in creation and making it shine forth in all human activities.

THE FIRST REDISCOVERY OF ORDINARY LIFE: THE REFORMATION

Now and then you hear it said that the idea of Christian affirmation of the world and ordinary life sketched here, and especially the positive evaluation of professional work, is only a
rather belated catching up with something accepted outside
the Catholic Church ever since the Reformation. We are told
that the Protestant work ethic, especially that of Calvinism
and Puritanism, long ago discovered the value of ordinary life
and the importance of professional work.

Is that true? I would say it is true *in part*, but also partly
not true. The Reformers did rediscover ordinary life and
work as a Christian vocation, and thereby they played a
major part in the formation of our modern world. But the
real heart of the Protestant rediscovery of the Christian
value of ordinary work (in Catholic apologetics, often
unjustly undervalued or even ignored) can, in my opinion,

---

4. See the homily "Freedom, a gift of God," in *Friends of God*, nos. 23–38.

only be saved and in the long run made fruitful within the totality of the Catholic faith.

Just here lies the historical and (I think) also ecumenical significance of the message and life of Josemaría Escrivá. Within the Catholic Church he is a kind of pioneer in the recovery of the original dimension of Christianity revolving around the common priesthood of the faithful and the fundamental equality all of the baptized inasmuch as they are called to holiness,[5] as those realities were first rediscovered by the reformers in their rebellion against the self-understanding and practice of the medieval Church.

At the same time, however, with Escrivá this was a recovery of an original dimension of Christianity *based on the foundation of the fullness of the Catholic faith*, as the Second Vatican Council confirmed it to be in making it official Catholic teaching. What is true and acceptable in this basic position of the reformers became mired in fateful difficulties—more or less understandable in historical terms—due to their abandoning the foundation of Catholic faith. Aspects of Reformation thinking that were historically among the most powerful were undoubtedly partly to blame for calling into existence a modern worldview that more and more considers itself to be the adversary of a religious worldview and way of life. Yet one should not ignore the fact that many forms of Protestantism have produced spiritual fruit that even today supplies countless Christians with inner support and a religious orientation.

What was the so-called basic concern of the Reformers and their followers?

It is best understood against the background of the medieval image of the Church and Christian life. To put it in very simplified and somewhat sketchy terms, the Christian

---

5. In this regard see Kurt Koch, "*Kontemplativ mitten in der Welt, Die Wiederentdeckung des Taufpriestertums beim seligen Josemaría Escrivá*," in César Ortiz (ed.) *Josemaría Escrivá, Profile einer Gründergestalt* (Cologne, 2002): pp. 311–327.

world was, for medieval man, divided into two groups. One was composed of the clergy and religious, who were responsible for what pertained to spiritual things and salvation. They renewed the sacrifice of Christ in Holy Mass. They dispensed the sacraments, they prayed and sacrificed through mortification and works of penance and charity. They were the Christians in the full sense, living their Christianity as a vocation. The priests were the middlemen between the world and God; while the members of religious orders, who through their rejection of the world gave themselves completely to God, kept the ship of the Church afloat by their spiritual lives. On the other side were the laity, who were responsible for earthly things. They labored in the fields and the workshops and fought in the wars. Through good works, alms, and pious foundations they made it possible for the priests to say Mass and the monks and nuns to pray and do penance, while they themselves concentrated on the needs of this world. The Church was the ship, the clergy and religious did the rowing, the laity were the passengers.

By the time of the Reformation, however, the ship of Peter had gotten rather leaky, and the rowers were too tired or lazy or simply too weak to make headway. There were understandable grounds at the time for wondering whether the traditional division of labor was still meaningful or whether it was not even basically the problem—whether the bad state of the clergy and religious and the Church as a whole resulted from this unholy division of labor. Shouldn't all Christians feel themselves responsible for the progress of the ship? Why should it be precisely the ones who kept the world moving—workers of every sort, farmers, craftsmen, statesmen, scientists, artists—who should consider themselves only passengers on this particular voyage? Why should it be those who withdraw from all the demands and necessities of life who are most pleasing to God?

In a sense, the reformers all rejected in one way or another the idea that in the Church there should be people like those belonging to the priestly state who, in a special way and employing special powers provided by Christ, were responsible for everyone's salvation. As a result, they threw all mediating structures overboard. There would be no more ministerial priesthood in the traditional sense, no sacraments, and, especially, no Mass. In this sense, the ship with passengers was done away with. After the Reformation, each person was to stand directly before God, needing no one else to pray for him, do penance and offer sacrifice for him, or remit his sins. Faith alone provides direct contact with the Redeemer, and one is saved through this faith. Each one now sits in his own boat and has to row himself, as "priest of his own life"[6]— where the boat is Christ and the oars one's own faith.

The church community and the sacraments are still there, of course, but only to nourish this faith and provide an expression of it. "The church" is no longer truly an instrument of salvation, but only a symbol of salvation; it is the visible community of the called. For Luther, the church is the people of God assembled in the Holy Spirit, although he continued to recognize certain institutional aspects. In Calvinism, membership in the visible church remains a condition for life in the invisible community of those chosen by God.[7] But the foreground is now occupied by concern regarding the certainty of one's own salvation; and to have this certainty is now, so to speak, a product of one's own faith, which must be proven in one's daily life.

In this way, the circumstances of ordinary life—work, marriage, family life, social and civil duties—take on an eminently religious meaning. Inner morality is no longer sur-

---

6. I am purposely using here a formula which really comes from Escrivá: "Through baptism all of us have been made priests of our lives, 'to offer spiritual sacrifices acceptable to God through Jesus Christ' (1 Pet 2:5). Everything we do can be an expression of our obedience to God's will and so perpetuate the mission of the God-man." *Christ Is Passing By*, no. 96.

7. See the article "Kirche" in the *Lexikon für Theologie und Kirche*, 3rd ed. Freiburg i. B.: year 1993–2001, vol. 3 [condensed version in *Lexikon der Reformationszeit* (Freiburg, 2002): pp. 392 ff].

passed by monastic asceticism. Instead, as Luther and later the Calvinistic Puritans say, worldly duties are now themselves a "calling" to an activity in which God's will for each is shown and which is carried on not as a goal in itself, but for the glory of God, so that it must be made holy. For Luther, all men are now in a "spiritual state." The Protestant preacher Sebastian Franck sees the meaning of the Reformation as precisely that—now everyone has become a monk.

In Puritanism, then, the Protestant work ethic took on a special character. The Canadian philosopher Charles Taylor, in his book *Sources of the Self*,[8] spells out this connection and especially the self-understanding of the English and North American Calvinist Puritans; it is worth reading. Taylor writes: "Whereas in Catholic cultures the term 'vocation' usually arises in connection with the priesthood or monastic life, the meanest employment was a calling for the Puritans, provided it was useful to mankind and imputed to use by God. In this sense all callings were equal, whatever their place in the social hierarchy."[9] In the seventeenth century, Joseph Hall[10] said that "God loveth adverbs; and cares not how good, but how well."[11] A thing done with love for God is done for his glory and is sanctified. "God does not look at the excellence of the accomplishment," wrote William Perkins[12] in the sixteenth century, "but at the heart of the worker." And then he added: "Now if we compare worke to worke, there is a

---

8. *Sources of the Self: The Making of the Modern Identity* (Cambridge, MA: 1989). I have taken the metaphor of the ship and its passengers from Taylor's book. Taylor for his part takes most of the footnotes [in this part of his book] from the following works: Edmund S. Morgan, *The Puritan Family* (New York: 1966); Perry Miller, *The New England Mind: The Seventeenth Century* (Cambridge, MA: 1967); and Charles H. George and Katherine George, *The Protestant Mind of the English Reformation* (Princeton: 1961).

9. Ibid., p. 223.

10. 1574–1656. He was raised under Puritan influence, studied at Cambridge University, and finally became Bishop of Norwich and was deposed from his See by the Puritans.

11. Cf. *Sources of the Self*, p. 224.

12. Perkins lived from 1558 to 1602.

difference betwixt washing of dishes, and preaching of the word of God: but as touching to please God none at all . . . yea deedes of matrimonie are pure and spirituall . . . and whatsoever is done within the lawes of God though it be wrought by the body, as the wipings of shoes and such like, howsoever grosse they appear outwardly, yet are they sanctified."[13]

Through sin the right order was turned upside down and man became a slave of created things. For the Puritan, therefore, the lives of people living in the world, especially their marriages and their work, are realities that God has willed and from which no one ought to remove himself. The challenge is to use these realities, not out of love for the world, but only out of love for God. From this, to quote Joseph Hall again, comes the project of human life: "to serve God in the serving of men in the works of our callings."[14] Besides Calvinistic Puritanism, Lutheranism and, later, Pietism and Methodism also rediscovered the Christian value of ordinary life. In more recent times, this has been the basis of an activist Christianity characterized by faith-based charitable and social engagement.[15]

THE PROTESTANT WORK ETHIC, RELIGIOUS MOTIVATION, AND THE SIGNATURE OF THE MODERN

From the beginning, however, this rediscovering had a weak spot. Misunderstanding the call to the religious life as contempt for the laity, the reformers believed that the only way to restore the laity's true value, as well as to recognize the common priesthood of the faithful, was to do away with religious life and with the ministerial priesthood. This radical rejection of the asceti-

---

13. *Sources of the Self*, p. 224.

14. Ibid., pp. 225.

15. See in this regard Gerhard A. Ritter, *Der Sozialstaat: Entstehung und Entwicklung im Internationalen Vergleich*, 2nd ed. (Munich: 1991): pp. 36ff. Ritter notes, however, that in Catholic areas help for the poor, in reaction to the Reformation, was understood much sooner as an ecclesiastical-religious undertaking.

cal monastic renunciation of the world and of apostolic celibacy arose from a curious one-sidedness in its emphasis on the secularity of human life. At the same time, paradoxically, the reformers were also of the opinion that the world and mankind were radically corrupted by sin. Only through faith could salvation from this corruption take place and life in this world become something pleasing to God—though without the inner corruption of earthly things being overcome. Here arose a curious ambivalence and tension, between a radical turning *toward* the world as a God-willed reality and salvation *from* the world as a fallen, sin-filled state of disorder.

Neither the Lutheran idea of work as "profession" nor the Calvinist-Puritan idea of the sanctification of work was really aimed at the redemption of the world and thereby at its inner healing and sanctification. "Salvation," according to Reformation teaching, takes place only on the plane of belief in Christ as Savior, who saves man from his sinful situation without healing him inwardly. In Luther, work is a command of God directed to the rich as well. But work itself continues to be considered in accord with the tradition received from monastic asceticism, as when Luther writes: "Do not be lazy and useless, nor trust either in your own work and activity, but work and do things, yet, nevertheless, expecting everything from God." Work should be useful and profitable, but the important thing is that it be an opportunity to strengthen one's trust in God. The Christian works and abandons his concerns in God.[16] The Lutheran vision of work and of one's profession grows increasingly providentialistic, leading to passive acceptance of life's concrete circumstances and the indications one receives as the will of God. Only the pietism of the eighteenth century brought a certain correction.

For its part, neither did the Calvinistic view of the world reach any interior reconciliation of the world with God,

---

16. See Werner Conze, article "Arbeit," in *Geschichtliche Grundbegriffe*, vol. I (Stuttgart: 1972): p. 163.

actuated by Christ with the collaboration of man. Rather, there arose an effort to cover the corruption of the world (and of the great number of people not destined to salvation who arouse God's rejection by their way of life and who are, in any case, lost) with a kind of order corresponding with the commandments of God, and in this way to render him glory. As a result, Calvinistic ecclesiastical institutions were always instruments of coercion and domination while often simultaneously developing a revolutionary dynamism. Absent a true interest in the "salvation of the world," there is naturally a profound ambivalence in the Puritan conception, which invites one to use the goods of this world solely for the glorification of God, but without enjoying them, since that enjoyment is a false love of the world injurious to love of God and the salvation of souls.

In his famous study *The Protestant Ethic and the Spirit of Capitalism*[17] (still a subject of controversy), the German sociologist Max Weber in 1902 tried to show that the Protestant ethic of work became—largely unintentionally, as Weber points out—an enormous force for economic activity that transformed the world. The Puritan work ethic demanded a commitment to the world, diligence, and observance of the principle of usefulness. The systematic and rationalistic way of life of the Puritan—Weber coined the term *innerweltliche Askese* ("worldly asceticism")—a search for success, gain, and riches, was seen now as a sign and means of divine election and personal salvation. For, as the Puritan pastors preached, how could one be diligent, honest, and effective in one's work and profession, except that one had been renewed and chosen in Christ? The true Christian is the one who is useful to the community and to the world, for in this way the glory of God is increased. Here a morality of effort and success comes into view, a utilitarian morality, although an ascetic one, and

---

17. Max Weber, *The Protestant Ethic and the Spirit of Capitalism*, translated by Talcott Parsons (New York: Charles Scribner's Sons, 1930).

endowed with a purely religious foundation. And by the back door, so to speak, it seems to bring back into play the "justification by works" that was rejected by the Reformation.[18]

Calvin himself, says Weber, rejected the idea that one could deduce from exterior behavior anything about a person's election by predestination. But the Calvinists who followed him thought very differently. They saw good conduct in life as a sign of predestination. The good works did not produce the salvation, however, but are only a sign of having been chosen. Of course there were other motivations for this "worldly asceticism" of the Puritan work ethic, as for example a notable apocalyptic belief that the end of the world was close at hand.[19] But all came together in an inseparable unity of work, diligence, success, consciousness of one's own salvation, and the glorification of God.

The effort to gain riches was to be rejected, yet it was understood that riches that come from work are a blessing of God. And the desire for gain was considered legitimate, even the ambition to attain all that could be useful from a practical point of view and would help progress; at the same time, unlimited enjoyment of what one had gained was not allowed. The preacher John Cotton[20] wrote in the seventeenth century about the "holy Christian man": "diligence in worldly business and yet deadness to the world . . . a man to take all opportunities to be doing something, early and late, and looseth no opportunity, go any way and bestirr himself

---

18. This shift to an ethic of diligence and success should be seen as a slow and progressive change. In William Perkins, and generally in the Puritanism described by Charles Taylor, there seems to be more of a Christian ethic based on attitude; see, for example, Perkins: "God does not value the excellence of the effort, but the heart of the one working" (Taylor, op. cit., p. 550, note 30.)

19. Cf. Hartmut Lehmann, "*Asketischer Protestantismus und ökonomischer Rationalismus: Die Weber-These nach zwei Generationen,*" in Wolfgang Schluchter (ed.) *Max Webers Sicht des okzidentalen Christentums: Interpretationen und Kritik* (Frankfurt a. M.: 1988): pp. 529–553.

20. 1585–1652; educated at Trinity College, Cambridge. In 1633 he immigrated to the Massachusetts Bay Colony and until his death was "teacher" at the First Church of Boston.

for profit, this will he do most diligently in his calling, and yet be a man dead-hearted to the world. . . . Though he labor most diligently in his calling, yet his heart is not set upon these things."[21]

This worldly asceticism finally led to the dilemma formulated by John Wesley, the founder of Methodism, in the following manner: religion produces industriousness and a spirit of saving, but these in their turn produce riches and encourage "pride, passion, and love of the world in all of its forms," which is injurious to religion. Wesley came to the conclusion that to amass treasure in heaven men need to earn as much as they can, save as much as they can, and give as much as they can.[22] In the era of industrialization, nevertheless, the Puritan work ethic and its imperative to work, gain, and save, while ruling out enjoyment, led also to the identification of the interests of God with the interests of employers. The worker, who had no possessions but multiplied the employer's riches by his labor, could count on his predestination. The unequal division of the goods of this world became a "work of divine providence."[23]

In sum, the Protestant inclination toward the world and ordinary life did not add up to a true affirmation of the world, either in its Lutheran or Puritan-Calvinistic form. In fact, neither Luther nor the Calvinists managed to understand the Redemption as a re-establishment of creation or a "new creation" in Christ. Redemption and salvation always meant the redemption and salvation of the individual, although the individual in turn was integrated into the ecclesial community formed by faith. The work ethic of the Puritans was no more than a means of transcending the world through a religious

---

21. Taylor, op. cit., p. 223.

22. Weber, op. cit., pp. 175–176.

23. Ibid. p. 177f. Note that such views also existed on the Catholic side. A truly theologically motivated social teaching directed to bettering the situation of the working class, nevertheless developed in the nineteenth century, at first mainly in the Catholic world (for example, through Antoine-Frédéric Ozanam in France and Bishop von Ketteler of Mainz in Germany).

attitude in order to be able to direct oneself to God and increase his glory in the midst of the activities and conditions of this world and ordinary life. In a certain sense, it was a secularized version of the ideal of monastic asceticism. It is not the world that is redeemed but only the individual, who in the end separates himself from the world. Work and one's profession are the occasion and means for sanctifying oneself, and attaining the salvation of one's own soul.

The Puritan's inclination to the world did not derive from a love that affirms its radical goodness as a work created by God and an authentic interest in its salvation from the corruption of sin. For this reason, despite impulses and motives that were profoundly Christian, the religious foundation of this ethos is fragile. There is no intrinsic relationship between work and Redemption.

If the religious roots and the resulting motivations are defective, what remains is a work ethic that can be open only to worldly perspectives. Benjamin Franklin's utilitarian idea of diligence is an instance. "Time is money" was his classic formulation. One aspires to a way of life in the highest degree rational, though not directed primarily to the increase of possessions or pleasure—the secularized and irreligious Puritan is no hedonist—but simply the increase of one's own abilities and capacity for action, of which acquiring money and accumulating wealth in a legal manner are signs[24] (hence the well-known maxim of Franklin calling for the renunciation of sexual activity except for purposes of generation and health). This ethic revolved around productive honesty and the glorification of professional duties. It doesn't seem possible to construct an authentic theology and spirituality of ordinary life, and of work in particular, on this foundation.

The final collapse of the unity between the work ethic and its religious motivation contributed significantly to the peculiar

---

24. Weber, op. cit., p. 52ff.

character of the modern world. Secularism and religious consciousness began to flow in different streams and finally became alienated from each other. The disappearance of the religious basis gave rise to a process of secularization. With the religious element discarded like a suit that had grown too small, we once more had a world of work saturated with economic rationality and progressive productive efficiency but closed to all transcendence. Re-establishing a connection between everyday life (in particular, ordinary professional work) and a loving relationship between us and God and our task as disciples of Christ became impossible and eventually came to seem superfluous.

Finally, this rediscovery of ordinary life led to its despiritualization and, often, its dehumanization (even though science, technology, and modern medicine have had historically unprecedented humanitarian results). Christian faith and life in the world, with all its preoccupations and expectations, are traveling in parallel channels out of touch with each other—when, that is to say, Christian life does not simply dissolve into pure social commitment or political activism.

HUMAN WORK IN CHRISTOLOGICAL PERSPECTIVE. THE "SECOND REDISCOVERY" OF ORDINARY LIFE: JOSEMARÍA ESCRIVÁ

The reformers wanted to turn the Church upside down. But would it not have been better to give it back its lost foundation—to rediscover the universal call to sanctity and the sanctifying value of ordinary life in the middle of the world, on the basis of "a Gospel of Work"?

This would have meant, in the first place, maintaining the essential Catholic tradition: the Church as the great ship in which we can all be saved; by our faith naturally, though not by the works of our faith but only and uniquely by the works of Jesus Christ and by his merits. The ship of the Church is constructed of these merits, which reach us through the

Church's sacraments, especially through the making-present of the Sacrifice of the Cross in the celebration of the Eucharist, Holy Mass. In this way—and here is the quintessence of the "sacramental logic"—the merits of Jesus are converted into our personal merits, human insufficiency and debility are overcome by the salvific divine action.

In the second place, it would have required admitting that salvation in Christ (in short, the Christian life) does not mean only being saved by faith from one's own sinfulness and that of the world. It includes the restoration, the healing, of the order of creation in its fullness, and with that, its sanctification through the love of Christ that, as Paul says in his letter to the Romans, "has been poured into our hearts through the Holy Spirit."[25]

It is a curious fact that even in the Catholic Church the power of custom was so great that even genuine Catholic belief in the basic goodness of the world did not give rise to a theology of work or of ordinary life in general.[26] While the relationship between faith and world forged by Protestantism, and the "work ethic" arising from it, undoubtedly fostered a process of secularization, a parallel if not entirely opposed structure of faith and life in the world, the burden of the Catholic medieval tradition, gave rise to a no less explosive conflict between faith and the modern world. The result up until the Second Vatican Council was rejection of "the modern" in some of its characteristic aspects such as freedom of religion, conscience, and the press, as well as a deep suspicion

---

25. Rom 5:5.

26. For example, in St. Francis de Sales's book *Introduction to the Devout Life*, which was aimed at lay people, there is no chapter on work. I believe a real "theology of work" only began to develop in the 1950s (e.g., with M.-Dominique Chenu), along with a positive view that saw human work not as "punishment" but as the original vocation of man (cooperation in God's creative work). The state of such reflection at that time can be found in the second edition of the *Lexikon für Theologie und Kirche* (ed. by Karl Rahner), Vol. I, Article *"Arbeit: II. Theologisch,"* by Henri Rondet (Freiburg i. B.: year 1957): pp. 803ff. Here it is clear, to be sure, that work on the one hand and contemplation and prayer on the other are sharply divided, even when, through both of them, "the praise of God resounds."

of the *ethos* of modern political culture[27] and the reality of the modern world of work and economics (anti-capitalism, rejection of unionism, profit-seeking, and competition, along with a certain amount of socio-economic and politically motivated anti-Semitism).

As to the latter, this reaction against the modern world—against secularism, business ability, and the desire for profit—to a great extent was responsible for religiously, socially, and politically motivated anti-Semitism. This view, which frequently assumed the features of a conspiracy theory, saw the Jews as having destroyed the harmony of the old corporate-feudalistic Christian world by their profit seeking and competitiveness, their worldliness and materialism—in short, by their love of the world and its goods, which was opposed to the Christian ideal of asceticism.[28] The emancipation of the Jews—giving them the full rights of citizenship—was seen as one of the ominous results of the French Revolution and liberalism.

The typically Catholic variety of the split between faith and the modern world involved widespread identification of the religio-ascetical ideal of perfection found among religious with the ideal of Christian life and a Catholic social and political order, and rejection of the modern and its turning to the world that was bound up with it, along with a deeply rooted mistrust of freedom and pluralism. Thus ordinary Christians, the laity, who were necessarily involved with things of this

---

27. Compare in this regard chapter 4 in this volume entitled "Truth and Politics in Christian Society."

28. This is how the magazine *La Civiltà Cattolica*, which was representative of the clerical-Catholic thinking of that period, put it in 1936: "*La questione Giudaica*," *La Civiltà Cattolica* IV, 1936, pp. 37–46 (the article apparently was written by Fr. Enrico Rosa). On page 45 the Church of the Middle Ages is spoken of in laudatory terms. Persecution of the Jews was always forbidden, and they were actually protected, but they were not granted the same civil rights as Christian citizens, "in order in this way to make them innocuous [*innocui*]." "Today too one must find ways suitable to modern conditions to make them innocuous, but of course without any kind of persecution." This was in accord with the traditional Church position which called for restricting Jews to ghettos and, after emancipation, for restricting their citizenship (this continued until the early 1940s), since they were thought to have a harmful influence on society and public life.

world, came to be seen as second-class Christians in regard to what concerned spiritual life and apostolic responsibility. Life in the world, work and a profession, as well as the duties of married life and family, were generally considered hindrances to a real spiritual life and striving for Christian perfection. Little or no attention was paid to the virtues connected with ordinary professional work—industriousness, dependability, honesty, and a healthy competitiveness—as elements of the spiritual life and expressions of Christian charity.

All attempts to bridge the gap between faith and the modern world, and overcome the growing separation between God and modern life, were based on initiatives directed to this world "from the outside" and also "from above," and so conducted in a clerical manner. At most, the laity were understood to be cooperators in the apostolate of the ecclesiastical hierarchy, while their spiritual life was reduced to appropriating bits and pieces from the spirituality of various religious orders. It was literally inconceivable in this view that the spiritual life and apostolic activity of ordinary Christians should come precisely "from the world" and "from their everyday life in it."

Just here is where the "Catholic rediscovery" of ordinary life by Josemaría Escrivá comes in. In his frequently quoted homily of 1967, which has been published under the title "Passionately Loving the World,"[29] he explained to students, faculty, and staff of the University of Navarra:

> The world is not evil, because it has come from God's hands, because it is His creation, because "Yahweh looked upon it and saw that it was good" (cf. Gen 1:7 ff). We ourselves, mankind, make it evil and ugly with our sins and infidelities. Have no doubt: any kind of evasion of the honest realities of daily life is for you, men and women of the world, something opposed to the will of God. On the contrary, you must understand now, more clearly, that God is calling you to

---

29. Cf. *Conversations*, nos. 113–123.

serve Him *in and from* the ordinary, material and secular activities of human life. He waits for us every day, in the laboratory, in the operating theatre, in the army barracks, in the university chair, in the factory, in the workshop, in the fields, in the home and in all the immense panorama of work. Understand this well: there is something holy, something divine, hidden in the most ordinary situations, and it is up to each one of you to discover it.[30]

This is not just saving oneself through faith from a world fallen through sin into a state of disorder and preserving the faith through a life of useful industriousness. Instead, Escrivá is appealing for the discovery of the holy, the divine, and the good, hidden in this world in ordinary work and everyday life. Here is a true love for the world—a correct love for and interest in this world and its situation and health. For the Christian, God is not only "beyond" the world; one also meets him *in* it.

Escrivá sees in work, as he wrote in 1954, the "dignity of life" and a "duty imposed on us by our Creator."[31] As the creation narrative in the Bible tells us, God created man in order to work. Work is not a result of man's falling into sin; it is not synonymous, as the medieval conception of work would have it, with exhaustion and pain, to which we must submit ourselves for the sake of survival and penance and in order to avoid laziness. It is a divinely willed task and vocation, which fundamentally defines man's identity in this world.

The ordinary daily work of each person—not only one's professional work but any honorable human activity—can be looked at under two aspects.

First of all, it is through this work that man takes part in the work of creation. Work is "the source of progress, of the building up of civilization and of prosperity." At the same

---

30. Ibid., no. 114.

31. Letter of May 31, 1954. Cited by José Luis Illanes, *La sanctificación del trabajo, tema de nuestro tiempo* (Madrid: 1966): p. 24f.

time, however, all of men's activities and doings require the purifying power of the Redemption. Therefore, "all things of this earth, including material creation, and the earthly and time-bound activity of men . . . have to be brought to God— and now, after sin, redeemed, forgiven—every single one in accord with its own nature, according to the immediate goal that God has conferred on each, but with the condition that it see its final, supernatural destination in Jesus Christ."[32] At this point Escrivá cites the Letter to the Colossians 1:19–20: "For in him all the fullness of God was pleased to dwell, and through him to reconcile to himself all things, whether on earth or in heaven, making peace by the blood of his cross."

This points clearly to a first and fundamental aspect: The Christian's love for the world, this basic, even passionate affirmation of the world, unites the love of God the Creator— "and God saw that it was good"—with the love of God the Redeemer, who wished to make creation shine forth in its original goodness as "a new creation in Christ." This became possible when the Son of God made man shed his blood on the cross for us—for the forgiveness of sins. "Passionate love for the world" is the love of the Creator pleased with the work that he brought forth out of nothing, especially mankind. It also is the love of the Savior, the love of Christ, which came to restore us men, and at the same time the whole of creation, to a condition of original goodness. And it is a redeeming love in which every Christian takes part through Baptism and the work of the Holy Spirit.

What we have here, then, are man and the world as God's creation redeemed by Christ. The "salvation of the world"

---

32. Letter of March 19, 1954, cited by Illanes, op. cit., p. 61f. See also Illanes "The Church in the World: The Secularity of Members of Opus Dei," in Pedro Rodríguez, Fernando Ocáriz, and José Luis Illanes, *Opus Dei in the Church: An Ecclesiological Study of the Life and Apostolate of Opus Dei*, pp. 121–190; Fernando Ocáriz, "*Vocazione alla santità in Cristo,*" in Manuel Belda, José Escudero, José Luis Illanes, Paul O'Callaghan (eds.), *Santità e mondo* (Proceedings of the theological study conference on the teachings of Blessed Josemaría Escrivá, Rome: October 12–14, 1993), Vatican City: 1994, pp. 27–42, esp. pp. 39ff.; Giorgio Faro, loc. cit., p. 99ff.

and the "glory of God" converge. Christian life is not merely a matter of being saved from this fallen world by faith and a good conscience. It is the inner transformation of men and women in Christ, which must finally lead to an inner renewal and healing, even sanctification, of the world accomplished through God's grace.

This leads to the second aspect: The salvation of the world and the salvation of each person are inseparable. The sanctification of the world or of work requires and is intertwined with the sanctification of the person and his or her Christian perfection. Thus, as Escrivá says, since we by our work participate in God's creative work, "every task, of whatever kind it is, is not only fully worthy, but also a means for attaining human, earthly, and supernatural perfection. . . . We Christians have the duty of building up earthly society, both on the basis of love for all mankind and for our own personal perfection."[33]

"Personal perfection" means of course the perfection in love worked by the Holy Spirit in and through Christ—that is, Christian perfection and holiness, an ideal which for hundreds of years was linked to renunciation of the world, contempt for it, and monastic asceticism. When Escrivá speaks of Christian perfection, however, he is speaking also, and as an integral part of it, of human perfection: the many human and supernatural virtues, especially love, justice, wisdom, fortitude, and temperance, industriousness, magnanimity, humility, loyalty, inner detachment, together with professional competence, seriousness, a spirit of initiative, and so forth.

According to Escrivá, therefore, holiness is not to be found in turning away from the world, and even less is the secularity of mankind, particularly work, a hindrance or obstacle on the path to unity with God and perfection in love; on the contrary, it is a means and path to it. The Christian identifies himself with Christ's cross through the effort the

---

33. Letter of May 31, 1954, op. cit.

work requires, through acceptance of his own limitations, weakness, and mistakes, through the inner struggle against comfort, superficiality, and egoism, and through suffering the injustices and humiliation that often accompany striving for justice and moral integrity. Escrivá stressed again and again that this is an asceticism and a cross rich in human and supernatural fruitfulness. He liked to call it "smiling asceticism." "Be cheerful, always cheerful," he urged. "It is for those to be sad who do not consider themselves sons and daughters of God."[34]

This does not mean instrumentalizing work for ascetical purposes or a mere adaptation of the Benedictine motto "*ora et labora*" (pray and work). Along with maintaining the monastery, caring for the sick, and the hospitable care of pilgrims, in whom one should see Christ, work (manual labor and reading) has for the monk (at least in its basic form, according to the Benedictine rule) the ascetical purpose of warding off laziness.[35]

To be sure, the differences should not be exaggerated: what we have here is not always an absolute antithesis, but simply different points of view within a common Christian outlook. And yet the difference can be substantial. The Benedictine "*ora et labora*" effected an epochal revaluation of human work, especially manual work, together with the civilizing transmission of the heritage of ancient culture. But at least in its original intention, the Benedictine work ethic that so largely shaped Europe did not come from an interest in the world and its human and supernatural salvation and sanctification.

In a general sense, of course, the monk sought through his life of self-sacrifice and penance to provide spiritual, supernatural energy to the world, and in doing so he worked for its

---

34. Josemaría Escrivá, *Furrow*, no. 54.

35. Cf. *Die Regel des Heiligen Benedikt*, ch. 48 (Einsiedeln/Zürich: 1961): p. 97 ff. For the continuing significance of the Benedictine "*ora et labora*," see the remarks of Joseph Cardinal Ratzinger, *Gott und die Welt. Glauben und Leben in unserer Zeit. Ein Gespräch mit Peter Seewald* (Stuttgart/Münich: 2000): p. 334 ff.

inner renewal in Christ. It is precisely in this that one finds the deepest and essential meaning of the religious state for the Church. But *work*, our subject here, just did not have this significance for the monk. For almost a thousand years the Cistercians have referred to their prayer in choir as "Opus Dei," but they did not call their work that. Ultimately, therefore, service of God and work were seen as separate, parallel things rather than a spiritual unity.

The ordinary Catholic in the world needs to see professional work and everyday tasks in the family and society as a "work of God," *opus Dei*, and therefore as prayer rising like incense to God. Carried out with the creative and redemptive love of God, work itself becomes prayer. This is not just a matter of living piously in the world but in opposition to it, but of sanctifying the world—*consecratio mundi*—by transforming professional work and everyday life into "a work of God"—*operatio Dei, Opus Dei*.

DIVINE FILIATION AND THE UNITY OF WORK AND CONTEMPLATION

Here are the origins of a true spirituality of work. The concept of spirituality can, to be sure, lead one astray, since in the Catholic tradition it tends to signify either an ascetical way of living, apart from ordinary life, or a special way of living piously and finding God despite involvement in the tasks of this world—a way that parallels everyday life and in some way fills it out while at the same time correcting it.[36]

In this perspective, a spirituality of ordinary life like the one proclaimed by Josemaría Escrivá is not really a spirituality but a particular way of living in the world—a kind of spirit that is

---

36. To some extent this was the idea behind the "Third Orders" and confraternities that arose as early as the Middle Ages with the objective of enabling their members to live some aspects of religious spirituality in the world and in this way seek Christian perfection. A particular religious spirituality was adapted to the conditions of life in the world, often with social and charitable purposes also in view.

nothing else than the realization that as a baptized Christian one is called by God to be "another Christ," "Christ himself," in the place one occupies in the world. Part of it, too, is the consciousness of divine filiation that must pervade every human action, empowering us confidently to call God "Father." Part, too, is love for the cross as the means of salvation, along with surrendering oneself to the guidance of the Holy Spirit so as to fill every corner of life with the light of faith and the fire of Christ's love. This is not really a "spirituality for the laity," such as Francis de Sales promoted, but a "lay spirituality"[37] from the ground up: based on an understanding of the human reality of the ordinary Christian as a divine vocation.[38]

Basically, therefore, a Christian's ordinary life is the life of a child of God and thus also a contemplative life in which professional work, ascetical struggle, and contemplation are fused into a unity. As Josemaría Escrivá writes, "Christian faith and calling affect our whole existence, not just a part of it," so that each person's human vocation is an important part of his or her divine vocation as a Christian.[39] Work especially "is born of love; it is a manifestation of love and is directed toward

---

37. This is how it was formulated by Cardinal Albino Luciani (later Pope John Paul I) in an article about the Founder of Opus Dei in the July 25, 1978 issue of the Venetian newspaper *Il Gazzettino* under the title "*Cercando Dio nel lavoro quotidiano*" (Seeking God through Everyday Work).

38. This is why, to take one example, assigning a central importance to care for "little things" (see, for instance, *The Way*, chapter on "Little Things") is thoroughly traditional. For Escrivá, however, this is not, as it was in previous spirituality, a kind of spiritual exercise; it is first of all a recognition that not only the ordinary life of work of someone living in the world but also his or her social relationships and human love are ordinarily made up of little things and small details. Aside from this, Escrivá's teaching often intersects with various forms of Christian spirituality: for example, the great value he places on meditation on the most holy humanity of Jesus, for whose discovery he thanks St. Teresa of Avila, or the "spiritual childhood" of which St. Thérèse of Lisieux is surely the godmother. Escrivá has dipped deeply into the general fund of the tradition of Catholic spirituality, especially from the Fathers of the Church. His originality seems to me to reside in the fact that he conceptualizes Christian spirituality starting from ordinary life itself, rather than applying a spirituality to ordinary life so that the laity *too* can strive for Christian perfection *even though* they live in the world.

39. *Christ Is Passing By*, no. 46.

love. We see the hand of God, not only in the wonders of nature, but also in our experience of work and effort. Work thus becomes prayer and thanksgiving, because we know we are placed on earth by God, that we are loved by him and made heirs to his promises. We have been rightly told, 'In eating, in drinking, in all that you do, do everything for God's glory.'"[40]

This plainly calls for more than just thinking about God while working, saying a prayer, having a good intention. As we have said, work itself must become prayer, a raising of the heart to God, and this in turn means it must correspond to the logic of God's creative love: "And God saw that it was good." The work has to be good. It is not enough therefore to live piously in the midst of the world. One must give one's life with Christ to building up the world anew, in Christ: to working with Christ's love. Not that one must do "great" or "important" things. The opportunity for that seldom arises, while ordinary life usually is a mix of small things—which nevertheless can indeed be made great and meaningful for the salvation of the world through one's love for God and one's fellow men. God puts the greatness there when we bring the love of Christ into the daily routine. In a poetic flight, Escrivá proclaimed: "Heaven and earth seem to merge, my sons and daughters, on the horizon. But where they really meet is in your hearts, when you sanctify your everyday lives."[41]

For Escrivá, the model for this was to be found in the thirty years of Jesus' hidden life in Nazareth. "The fact that Jesus grew up and lived just like us shows us that human existence and all the ordinary activity of men have a divine meaning." These years, "which made up the greater part of Jesus'

---

40. Ibid., no. 48.

41. Homily, "Passionately Loving the World," in *Conversations*, no. 116. Like many others who tried to strengthen lay spirituality, Friedrich von Hügel (1852–1925) [a prominent Catholic thinker who spent most of his life in England], sought to bring spiritual life and everyday reality closer together. But we fail to find in his thought the decisive breakthrough: drawing spiritual life directly from the ordinary realities

life among men, he lived in obscurity"; but in the light of faith, they are "full of light. It illuminates our days and fills them with meaning." Here then for ordinary Christians living in the world is "a call to shake off our selfishness and easygoing ways" and follow Christ with their whole heart.[42]

This is why Escrivá demands that we "materialize" our spiritual lives—that is, avoid living some kind of double life. Christian life is not just a matter of "going to church, taking part in sacred ceremonies, being taken up with ecclesiastical matters, in a kind of segregated world, which is considered to be the ante-chamber of heaven, while the ordinary world follows its own separate path."[43] This would be a sort of pseudo-Christianity. One either finds Christ in daily life or one does not find him at all. The little details of each day must be filled with the greatness of God, which Escrivá called "making heroic verse out of the prose of each day," for, as he said, "there is something holy, something divine, hidden in the most ordinary situations, and it is up to each one of you to discover it."[44] Through the unity with Christ graciously granted

---

of the life of someone living in the world. The result was a certain parallelism, with work and everyday life, etc., on the one side and religious life on the other. Ordinary life and professional work were hardly seen as an encounter with God, and nothing is said about "sanctifying work" and "sanctifying through work." There was an attempt to make possible the spiritual growth of people involved in "external, necessary, mechanical activity," and to bring them to contemplative prayer; cf. Friedrich von Hügel, *Andacht zur Wirklichkeit. Schriften in Auswahl* (Munich: 1952): p. 222. Although von Hügel calls for the realization of God's love precisely in "contact with the contingent" (cf. ibid., pp. 154f.), for him the "dedication to the attainment of the unending and eternal" means "a decisive turning away from all pursuit of the accidental and finite." "Worldly activity," and "the earthly" seem in the end incapable of a radical contact with "heaven" (ibid., pp. 156f.). In the passage of Escrivá just cited, however ("Heaven and earth seem to merge, my sons and daughters, on the horizon. But where they really meet is in your hearts, when you sanctify your everyday lives"), we see an obvious contrast. Escrivá was quite familiar with the assessments of lay spirituality of that era and he often spoke of them. He saw in them a well-justified search for the "unity of life" that he himself was proclaiming; but it was a search that often led Christians into an insoluble conflict, because it was so difficult to bring their lives in the world into harmony with their wish for a deep spiritual life.

42. *Christ Is Passing By*, nos. 14–15.

43. *Conversations*, no. 113.

44. Ibid., nos. 116, 114.

to it, the world will become a way of God very much as "man is the way for the Church," as John Paul II put it in his inaugural encyclical, *Redemptor Hominis*, in 1979.[45]

"Holiness" is not reduced to worldliness, however, nor seen as the fruit of purely human activity. This is not at all some sort of redemption through work, but much more a redemption *of* work—the raising of everyday life to the level of the life of grace, the supernatural level. As Josemaría Escrivá sees it, we human beings do not bring this world to God through our work and achievements; rather, Christ "draws it to himself" when we struggle to set his cross at the summit of all our human activities—that is, when we do what we do with the love of Christ.[46]

The Christian can do this, inasmuch as he is a passenger in the common ship of the Church, and through it and Christ's priesthood present in it—that is, through the sacraments—repeatedly receives the saving, strengthening power of the grace of the Holy Spirit, Christ's love for his heavenly Father. In this way, life in the world becomes an experience of purification carried out through the merciful grace of God by identifying with Christ and his saving offering on the Cross and making a pleasing offering to God. The common priesthood of the faithful draws upon the strength of the priesthood of Christ, which the ordained ministerial priesthood and the sacraments make effectively present in the Church. Once more we have the great common ship, only now everyone mans the oars. And at the same time everyone is a passenger as well, including priests, bishops, and the pope. As baptized faithful, all are equal.

---

45. *Redemptor Hominis*, no. 14.
46. Cf. *Christ Is Passing By*, no. 183.

ASCETICAL AND ECCLESIOLOGICAL CONSEQUENCES: THE CHURCH AS "SHIP OF THE WORLD," FREEDOM AND PERSONAL RESPONSIBILITY

"Affirmation of the world" and "love for the world" seems to contradict that Christian view, so frequently repeated in the Bible, of the world as an enemy of souls, a temptation and adversary of God.[47] Are not love for the world and love for God in irreconcilable conflict? The Puritan ethic of sanctification of work arose from this opposition and from the attempt to lead love of the world in the right direction through love of God—a correct attitude directed solely to the glory of God. Love for the world therefore was always seen as a danger—the precondition for true love of God was thought to lie in distancing oneself from the world, even regarding it with contempt.[48]

Josemaría Escrivá is not a representative of this "worldly asceticism." The Puritan ethic of the sanctification of ordinary life always reflected genuinely Christian motives, especially the Pauline maxim that one should use the world as though one did not make use of it, since the form of this world was passing away.[49] Escrivá, however, stressed the other side of the coin: The world is plainly and simply good, because it originates in God's creative love. It is evil—men's antagonist and in a true sense fleeting—only insofar as it is marked by sin, which comes from the heart of man. Overcoming and suppressing this deformation is precisely the meaning of the Redemption through Christ in which every Christian is called through baptism to cooperate.

Thus for Escrivá true love of God means—and this is probably the decisive point—not overcoming the world, nor

---

47. Cf. in this connection see chapter 1 of this volume, "Josemaría Escrivá and Love for the World."

48. Taylor, p. 394.

49. Cf. 1 Cor 7:31.

even less having contempt for it, but precisely a certain kind of love for it. This love participates in the redemptive love of Christ, which overcomes sin. "Love for the world" for Escrivá therefore means entering this world in a new way, namely, Christ's way.

Many themes of Christian asceticism follow in its train, without life becoming a "worldly asceticism." Ordinary life, with its multiple tasks relating to profession, family, social life, and marital and family love, is both the mission of man and woman redeemed by Christ and at the same time a means and path of unity with God. Work that has become prayer and is at the same time service to others and an offering to Christ, is a way of inner purification, a loving acceptance of the cross of Christ, a way of true mysticism. It is union with God through the action of the Holy Spirit. This is what is called holiness, and its growth to maturity requires a lifetime in which there are periods of pain, with often heroic phases of self-denial, humiliation, inner detachment, and darkness, but also times of joy and inner peace for those who know they are children of God.[50]

At the same time, precisely from this happy union with God and this personal struggle for holiness and growth in the various virtues, arises the transformation of the world. Spiritual life in combination with a quite normal manner of engaging the world—in and through secularity, that is— becomes the vehicle for permeating all earthly realities with the spirit of Christ, renewing them from within, and building what Pope Paul VI called a "civilization of love." Writes Escrivá, "That is the calling of Christians that is our apostolic task, the desire which should consume our soul: to make this kingdom of Christ a reality, to eliminate hatred

---

50. A key text for this ascetical program is the homily "Towards Holiness" in Josemaría Escrivá, *Friends of God*, nos. 294–316. The texts for the Liturgy of the Hours (Office of Readings) for the memorial of St. Josemaría Escrivá are taken from this homily.

and cruelty, to spread throughout the earth the strong and
soothing balm of love."[51]

In just this way the mission of the Church in the world
reaches its goal. The Church is not only the ship that carries
mankind to eternal salvation, but it also is the ship of the
world, insofar as the members of the Church keep the world
afloat through their ordinary life and through the exercise of
their free, personal responsibility rather than as the long arm
of the ecclesiastical hierarchy. Just here lay men and women
become not mere passengers but also sailors, machinists, rowers, captains, and helmsmen—all these things, of course, with
the freedom of children of God, so that freedom and personal
responsibility are a substantial part of the normal makeup of
ordinary life. In work, society, family, or politics, everywhere,
Christians—in inner unity with the Church and with consciences formed in a Christian way—stand on their own feet
and act autonomously and on their own responsibility. Escrivá
offered no solutions for the problems of the world except this

---

51.*Christ Is Passing By*, no. 183. The text that summarizes this matter continues:

"Let us ask our king today to make us collaborate, humbly and fervently, in the
divine task of mending what is broken, of saving what is lost, of fixing what man has
put out of order, of bringing to his destination whoever has gone off the right road,
of reconstructing the harmony of all created things.

"Embracing the Christian faith means committing oneself to continuing Jesus
Christ's mission among men. We must, each of us, be *alter Christus, ipse Christus*:
another Christ, Christ himself. Only in this way can we set about this great undertaking, this immense, unending task of sanctifying all temporal structures from
within, bringing to them the leaven of redemption.

"I never talk politics. I do not approve of committed Christians in the world
forming a political-religious movement. That would be madness, even if it were
motivated by a desire to spread the spirit of Christ in all the activities of men.
What we have to do is put God in the heart of every single person, no matter who
he is. Let us try to speak then in such a way that every Christian is able to bear
witness to the faith he professes by example and word in his own circumstances,
which are determined alike by his place in the Church and in civil life, as well as
by ongoing events.

"By the very fact of being a man, a Christian has a full right to live in the world.
If he lets Christ live and reign in his heart, he will feel—quite noticeably—the saving
effectiveness of our Lord in everything he does. It does not matter what his occupa-
tion is, whether his social status is 'high' or 'low'; for what appears to us to be an
important achievement can be very low in God's sight; and what we call low or mod-
est can in Christian terms be a summit of holiness and service."

one: that Christians should see facing up to the world's problems as their task, with each one doing his or her share in the context of daily work and with the radical commitment required of one who follows Christ. Each must find his or her own specific solutions. "Ordinary life" also means: personal freedom, personally responsible use of one's rights as a citizen and as a worker, and seeing to it that the rights of others are respected.

In today's world the need to preserve the faith is becoming increasingly clear to Christians. Often, to be sure, that gives rise to a shallow demand for involvement in the world with Christian symbols as a kind of decoration or even to the insistence that the Church as an official institution has an actual political mandate, and never mind the legitimate freedom of the faithful. Escrivá's view on the contrary is that the Church, open to the world, should seek to renew that world from within, with its redemptive efficacy flowing from the ordinary lives of all the baptized in their work and activity in all areas of society.

Only through the inner renewal of persons through the grace of Christ, accomplished above all through the sacraments of the Church, the light of its teaching, and the working of the Holy Spirit in their hearts, can mankind renew the world. That is the indispensable Catholic pillar of Escrivá's rediscovery of ordinary life. The goal is not, however, to bring about salvation through work and one's personal achievements—as some Reformation thinking seems to suppose—but to open oneself to God's grace and the redemptive action of God in one's daily work. Thus Christ, through our solidarity with him, "will draw all things to himself,"[52] and so establish his reign, which, to be sure, will be definitively confirmed only at the end of times, at his second coming, that is, as a gift.

---

52. Jn 12:32; cf. *Christ Is Passing By*, no. 183.

CHAPTER 3

The New Evangelization and Political Culture

NOTES ON THE THEME OF FUNDAMENTALISM,
INTEGRALISM, AND OPUS DEI

MEDIATION OF TRUTH AND FREEDOM AS A POLITICAL-THEOLOGICAL PROBLEM

According to Peter Hertel, Opus Dei aims to bring about a "Christian baptism of society, where there would scarcely be room for a broad ideological pluralism, and those who think differently would be excluded as heretics."[1] Obviously this is a rash statement; but it is also the most interesting reproach that could be directed at Opus Dei. I believe one cannot avoid considering it, since it points to a real problem and one that I would not claim Opus Dei has already sufficiently dealt with. All the same, I do not see this as a question specifically for Opus Dei; rather it is a question for the universal Church—particularly now, when a new evangelization is urged.

---

1. Peter Hertel, "Opus Dei," in Wolfgang Beinert, ed., *Katholischer: Fundamentalismus, Häretische Gruppen in der Kirche?* (Regensburg: 1991): pp. 148–165. (Cf. also p. 171: "*Hinweise zur Entstehung der einzelnen Beiträge.*") See also the same author, *Ich verspreche euch den Himmel. Geistlicher Anspruch, gesellschaftliche Ziele und kirchliche Bedeutung des Opus Dei*, 2nd ed. (Düsseldorf: 1990): p. 67. For the doubtful source of Hertel's information see Hans Thomas, "*Zur Inszenierung der Medienkritik am Opus Dei,*" in Klaus Martin Becker/Jürgen Eberle, *Die Welt–eine Leidenschaft. Charme und Charisma des Seligen Josemaría Escrivá* (St. Ottilien: 1993): pp. 132–156. (See also "Origins of the Chapters in this Volume.")

The problem can be formulated more exactly as a problem of the mediation between truth and freedom, specifically the socio-political freedom of the individual.

The firmness of the magisterium of the Church in regard to the teachings of the faith and clearly defined certainties seems to touch all of society, and through its new evangelization and "Christianization" seems incompatible with social pluralism—or, more precisely, incompatible with a political culture resting on respect for freedom, that is, on the primacy of protecting the rights of the person against a so-called "right of truth." But not only is such a political culture of freedom based on a pre-existing social pluralism; it also produces necessary pluralistic consequences. Thus many consider it now unavoidable "to carry into the Church itself those (republican) principles developed in modern times for the relationship between religious bodies, such as autonomy, openness to the public, and balancing of interests."[2]

But this way of escaping the danger of becoming a fundamentalist ghetto Church closed off from the pluralistic modern world would not be practical. For the post-Vatican II Church, renouncing the Christianization of society would be equivalent to declaring itself superfluous and surrendering its most essential self-definition, that of being "in Christ . . . in the nature of sacrament—a sign and instrument, that is, in communion with God and of unity among all men."[3] Someone who believes, despite everything, that the new evangelization and, if you will, the Christianization of society can succeed—and believes it because he believes that God continues to carry out the wonders and miracles of his love through the Church—will be increasingly curious to know what is meant in speaking of a future Christian society. That is especially so of someone who does not want to retreat from the

---

2. Hans Thomas, "Kirche im Pluralismus: Das Feindbild 'Fundamentalismus' ist ein Bumerang," in *Die Neue Ordnung* 46 (1992), no. 4, pp. 293–303. cit. p. 293.

3. Vatican II, Dogmatic Constitution on the Church, *Lumen Gentium*, no. 1.

path marked out by freedom in modern times or go back to the days before the Second Vatican Council, since he would consider either thing a substantial falling-off from the level reached by contemporary civilization.

POLITICAL CULTURE AND THE CHURCH: AN HISTORICAL OVERVIEW

The reception of the Second Vatican Council, a process involving the whole Church, has yet to be fully accomplished. The process has the character of a crisis, as befits its epochal importance. Part of it is a question that has not yet been exhaustively clarified from the theological point of view: what it means to affirm that every Christian should act with full responsibility in political and social life, respecting in particular the legitimate autonomy of the temporal order, while at the same time faithfully and obediently adhering to what the Church teaches to be obligatory for the Christian conscience in such matters.

So what does the Church say is obligatory in the field of social doctrine and, specifically, political ethics? Does it teach, for example, that civil law must be a faithful, juridically positive translation of moral law as interpreted by the Church in an authentic and obligatory way? Once society has been Christianized, will Catholic citizens and politicians, perhaps the majority by then, have to vote and legislate in accordance with what the encyclical on morality *Veritatis Splendor* decrees? Will Catholic moral law carry the weight of penal and civil law? Will public criticism and dissent in matters of faith and moral doctrine be considered an assault not only upon the ecclesial community but upon the civil-political society with its powers of coercion?[4] In short: does Catholic doctrine concerning the subordination of liberty to truth have

---

4. This problem is shown clearly by Emanuele Severino, "*Un'aureola al cittadino*," in *Il Sabato*, XVI, 44 (October 30, 1993), pp. 67–69.

an immediate moral-political relevance as well as a moral-theological character? Is civil and political freedom legitimate and defensible only insofar as it is subservient to the truth taught by the Church in an authentic way?[5]

In the course of history the Church has given very diverse answers to these and similar questions. But in the context of the democratic constitutional state, a precise answer, secular and modern, has taken shape through an extremely complex historical process, to the point that it has become part of our political culture.[6] This culture is now our natural habitation; we have all been formed in it, although with national variations. It is based on an *ethos* of freedom that arose as an *ethos* of peace: the search for peace and security gave rise to the sovereign territorial state of modern times. The need to guarantee individual freedom in the face of abuses of power led to the constitutional subordination of power to law, especially to human rights recognized as enforceable fundamental rights. The demand for equality of freedom was finally concretized in the democratic principle of general and equal voting rights, with the modern democratic constitutional state its result.[7]

The Church's position in this process was characterized by partly justified fears and mutual misunderstandings, but also by a far-reaching inability to differentiate the specific political core of the liberal constitutional state—especially in regard to its demand for religious freedom—from the relativistic denial of religious and ethical truth.[8] The Church

---

5. Some commentaries on *Veritatis Splendor* by Polish bishops give one the uneasy feeling that government by law is not an absolute value or that the law and moral norms must coincide (as reported by KIPA news agency, June 10, 1993).

6. For what follows, see for greater detail Martin Rhonheimer, "*Perché una filosofia politica? Elementi storici per una risposta,*" in *Acta Philosophica* I (1992), pp. 233–263.

7. Cf. Martin Kriele, *Einführung in die Staatslehre. Die geschichtlichen Legitimitätsgrundlagen des demokratischen Verfassungsstaates*, 4th ed. (Opladen: 1990); Giovanni Sartori, *The Theory of Democracy Revisited* (Chatham House: Chatham, NJ, 1987).

8. Cf. Walter Kasper, "*Religionsfreiheit als theologisches Problem,*" in Johannes Schwartländer, *Freiheit der Religion. Christentum und Islam under dem Anspruch der Menschenrechte* (Mainz: 1993): pp. 210–229. Josef Isensee, "*Die katholischer Kritik an*

tended to identify its concept of a Christian state with the idea of the absolutist monarchical (Catholic) states of the Restoration period. It remained tied to the view that, as religious and moral error is an evil for the soul, so also it is an evil for civil society, so that error should not be conceded a right to exist, even though it could be tolerated by the state for the sake of protecting higher goods, such as peace. But what is granted by toleration does not provide a basis for an enforceable right and supplies no protection against the abuse of power by the state. Rights are limitations on state sovereignty and constitutional guarantees of freedom.

From the historical-theological point of view, the process of reorienting the Church—a process that does not always proceed as a straight line—is still encumbered by the political Augustinianism[9] of the early and high Middle Ages. In fact, this is a misinterpretation of Augustine according to which the institutions of the *civitas terrena* (earthly city) are nothing but "a service subordinated to the kingdom of heaven":[10] that is to say, a this-worldly coercive power in the service of truth, virtue, and eternal salvation. This led first of all to a sacralization of earthly power, with temporal sovereigns understanding their mission as an ecclesial-priestly service, and later to the reversal of relationships through the "Papal Revolution" that was initiated in the last years of the eleventh century and reached its culmination with Pope Innocent III.[11]

The desacralization of political power and its parallel subordination to the pontifical *plenitudo potestatis* constituted a

---

den Menschenrechten. *Der liberale Freiheitsentwurf in der Sicht der Päpste des 19. Jahrhunderts,*" in Ernst-Wolfgang Böckenförde, Robert Spaemann, eds., *Menschenrechte und Menschenwürde. Historische Voraussetzungen—säkulare Gestalt— christliches Verständnis* (Stuttgart: 1987): pp. 138–174.

9. Henri Xavier Arquillière, *L'Augustinisme politique. Essai sur la formation des théories politiques du Moyen Age*, 2nd ed. (Paris: 1955).

10. St. Gregory the Great, *Epist. III*, 65.

11. For the concept "Papal Revolution," see Harold J. Berman, *Law and Revolution. The Formation of the Western Legal Tradition* (Cambridge, MA: 1983), pp. 85 ff.

process in which the freedom of the Church was directly in play; but this was the freedom of a Church which understood its task as that of creating a Christian *republic*, a unified Christian world under its own superior jurisdictional power, which is to say, under the power of the clergy. Curiously, this task was conceived as a purely spiritual-pastoral mission. The hierocratic ideas of the curial ecclesiastical jurists never conditioned the practice of the popes. But anyone who exercises jurisdiction in the political sphere, even if only on spiritual and pastoral grounds, and who makes use of the corresponding coercive power, cannot escape the logic of the political and is basically demanding sovereignty. The same thing happened later in the case of Bellarmine's doctrine of the *potestas indirecta* [indirect power of the Pope]. Thomas Hobbes was the first to emphasize this fact, via a biting critique that included the distinction between temporal and spiritual power.[12]

To put it simply, the political culture of the modern state and its specific legitimacy are a response to the attempt to develop a civilization of virtue and truth under the Church's direction, an attempt that always failed because of its internal contradictions and its rigidity.[13] Once religious divisions set in, the paradigm of the political primacy of religious truth, to which all religious groups had subscribed at first, led inevitably to a bellicose and bloody dead end. The process that eventually supplied a way out of this impasse began with the doctrine of tolerance within states advocated by the French *politiques* and with the *ad extra* formula *cuius regio eius religio* (the religion of the territory ruled shall be the religion of its ruler). This pressed the Church to adapt increasingly defensive positions, which translated into its making successive compromises with the modern state without substantially

---

12. Thomas Hobbes, *Leviathan*, chapter 42.

13. This attempt is documented in the famous decree of Innocent III, *Novit Ille* of 1204, in Aemilius Friedberg, *Corpus Iuris Canonici, Editio Lipsiensis Secunda* (Graz: 1955), col. 242–244. For a few excerpts, see also Martin Rhonheimer, *Perché una filosofia politica?* op. cit., p. 239.

surrendering the earlier ideal. The latest of these compromises is the practice, still followed, of negotiating concordats.

THE CHURCH AND POLITICAL CULTURE: DEVELOPMENTS IN THE CHURCH'S TEACHING

It is a commonplace to claim that, after so many adaptations provoked by confrontations, retreats, and weakening of the traditional teaching, including Leo XIII's teaching on tolerance, the Second Vatican Council, its way prepared by the magisterial recognition of human rights by John XXIII, marks the beginning of a new stage in doctrinal development. The decree on religious freedom assumes as its model for the safeguarding of the rights of the individual the idea of the modern constitutional state and the rule of law. The Church thus surrenders its traditional position that "error has no rights" in society. With this, it acknowledges the fact that, in political and juridical terms, neither truth nor error can possess rights, since only persons can do that; and that asserting the rights of truth in contrast to error, which lacks rights, leads to the political inequality of persons in regard to rights and freedoms: in other words, to the domination of some by others in the name of truth.

The Second Vatican Council therefore marks a real break in continuity of Church teaching. Yet, continuity also is maintained with the teaching that the individual's conscience must be guided by truth that he himself does not create. The new thrust resides in the political philosophy implicit in the social doctrine of the Church and in political ethics once it began to separate itself from the political-ethical tradition of Christian antiquity and to adopt the modern mode of thinking which assigns political primacy to the individual rather than to the "rights of truth."[14]

---

14. Rhonheimer, *Perché un filosofia politica?* op. cit., esp. pp. 250 ff.; and also Ernst-Wolfgang Böckenförde, *Religionsfreiheit. Die Kirche in der modernen Welt* (Schriften zu Staat-Gesellshchaft-Kirche Band III), (Freiburg i. B.: 1990). Recently the continuity has been stressed once more by Walter Kasper, *Religionsfreiheit als theologisches Problem*, op. cit.

As far as personal freedom in general is concerned, this conception, which expresses the ethos of modern political culture, was fully accepted for the first time in John Paul II's encyclical *Centesimus Annus*, specifically in the fifth chapter ("State and Culture"), a very important text that has not received the attention it deserves. While traditional Catholic teaching speaks of the "dignity of the state" and of state authority as an image of divine authority,[15] as John XXIII, citing Pius XII, still did (and thereby conferred on state power a consecration raising it to the category of privileged interpreter of the common good), *Centesimus Annus* no longer situates "the visible image of the invisible God" in the state but rather in the human person; thus it is the person, not the state or truth, that is "the natural subject of rights that no one may violate."[16] No longer is there talk of the "rights and obligations of the state," but of the rights and freedoms of the person or the citizen.

In contrast, the state is considered realistically as a human institution, susceptible to corruption, that should be subject to democratic control and to a pluralistic system of communications media lest power be usurped by cliques. John Paul II also adverts to the "the danger of fanaticism or fundamentalism among those who, in the name of an ideology which purports to be scientific or religious, claim the right to impose on others their own concept of what is true and good. Christian truth is not of this kind." Its path is that of respect for freedom.[17]

As a political ethos of freedom and peace, political culture rests finally on the specifically antifundamentalist recognition of political space as "a space of negotiation, of functional relativization [seeing things, for reasons of functionality, in

---

15. John XXIII, *Pacem in Terris*, no. 47.

16. John Paul II, Encyclical *Centesimus Annus*, no. 44. The American philosopher Russell Hittinger is right when he describes this as the most important reorientation of Catholic social teaching since *Rerum Novarum*; see Russell Hittinger, "The Pope and the Liberal State," in *First Things*, December, 1992, p. 33.

17. *Centesimus Annus*, no. 46.

relative terms], of the breakdown of unconditional demands."[18] The "fundamentalist" deduces precisely "from the fact that Truth knows no compromise," that "even when one carries out a compromise that plainly is correct, compromises as such are still always bad."[19]

Negotiation, viewing things from the standpoint of functionality in relative (not relativistic) terms, and the capacity for compromise: these are pervasive in the ethos and practice of parliamentary democracy to which both right and left have repeatedly refused to grant precisely because of this character of negotiation.[20]

THE CATEGORICAL FOUNDATIONS OF PLURALISM

Absolute convictions and certainties about salvation are foreign to civil society as a whole and to its institutional practices. Civil society should restrict itself to those final *political* values that make possible common life in peace, freedom, and justice. It can allow itself to be a Pantheon—a temple of all gods. But those who try to reproduce this "enlightened" pluralism in their own consciences will probably have no convictions of their own, much less consciences, and that eventually will be the end of the Pantheon. For it depends on ultimate, immovable convictions concerning the rights and value of the human person, and in just this way differs from all its predecessors.

Modern political culture's ethos of human rights and the democratic constitutional state has developed from a Christian foundation. It has sloughed off another political

---

18. Robert Spaemann, "Bemerkungen zum Begriff des Fundamentalismus," in K. Michalski, *Die liberale Gesellschaft. Castelgandolfo-Gespräche 1999* (Stuttgart: 1993): pp. 177–194, cit. p. 185.

19. Ibid., p. 183.

20. In this regard see Martin Rhonheimer, *Politisierung und Legitimitätsentzug. Totalitäre Kritik der parlamentarischen Demokratie in Deutschland* (Munich: Freiburg i. B.: 1979), or the article "Politisierung" in *Historisches Wörterbuch der Philosophie*, (ed. by J. Ritter and K. Gründer), vol. 7 (Basel: 1989): pp. 1075–1079.

culture, basically pagan, that was of Roman-imperial origin and that precisely in its "Christianized" form had internal contradictions.[21] Insofar as the Church in her concrete, historical form is always a child of her time, she believed right into the twentieth century that the traditional model, to which the model of absolute monarchy later was added, belonged to her essence. But today, in recognizing the political culture of human rights, she is finding her way back to her own origins.

It follows, however, that a political culture based on human rights still needs the Christian leaven to which it demonstrably owes its beginnings. It must be noted, though, that this leaven did not develop solely within the Catholic Church (recall the decisive contribution of Calvinistic Presbyterianism, which helped form the spirit of community in the American colonies), and the Church often did not recognize the leaven as her own. Yet, we must not forget that the Anglo-Saxon legal tradition, central to the development of the modern constitutional state, goes back to the high Middle Ages, while the right of resistance, whose institutionalization can be seen accompanying the constitutional state, is traceable to the early medieval era.

Precisely for this reason it seems plausible that the contemporary political ethos need not be viewed as something foreign to a Christian view of politics. Although it no longer can appeal directly to the truth of morality, it does require a certain political ethic that sees the role of politics not as being an agent of salvation, but as a way by which people with a variety of interests and convictions about what is true can live together in justice, freedom, and peace.[22]

---

21. This orientation toward the ancient Roman tradition was astonishingly clear in the writings of the last representative of preconciliar Catholic political teaching, Cardinal Ottaviani. Cf. Alfredo Ottaviani, *Institutiones iuris publici ecclesiastici*, vol. 2, 4th ed. (Vatican City: 1960): esp. pp. 46–77.

22. Cf. as a programmatic sketch and justification of such political ethic, my previously cited article "*Perché una filosofia politica?*" and also Bernhard Sutor, *Politische Ethik. Gesamtdarstellung auf der Basis der Christlichen Gesellschaftslehre* (Paderborn: 1991).

In this sense, the modern political ethos recognizes a necessary "multidimensionality" of ethics, and this is its strength. It does not concern itself with truth, but instead neutralizes the explosive potential of competing views of truth by political means. This neutralization program is itself morally motivated, through a political morality, which has its own practical moral truth and is an integral part of "simple" morality. The power of the state and of the legislator is limited by the inalienable rights of man. In order to remain part of political culture, however, these require the recognition that there is *a truth about mankind* from which every political culture draws life and which is politically inviolable—even if this political inviolability cannot itself be guaranteed. This truth includes the human relationship to the transcendent. The Church in fact "is at once a sign and a safeguard of the transcendent character of the human person."[23]

If modern democratic-constitutional political culture and the political ethos proper to it were without truth—if relativism was the last word here[24]—one could not defend it with conviction (as one does, for example, when considering the right to life of the unborn as opposed to the right of self-determination of those already born and assigns greater legal protection to the former).[25] The so-called pluralistic conscience that elevates pluralism to an absolute when declaring truth to be relative results in the destruction of the truth dimension of the political ethos of the modern.[26]

23. Vatican II, Pastoral constitution *Gaudium et Spes*, no. 76.

24. This point of view is represented in its most extreme form by Richard Rorty, for example in his essay "The Priority of Democracy to Philosophy," in Merrill D. Peterson and Robert C. Vaughan, eds., *The Virginia Statute for Religious Freedom* (Cambridge, MA: 1988): pp. 257–282.

25. Cf. the decision of the German Federal Constitutional Court in regard to abortion of May 28, 1992 in *Juristen Zeitung* (special edition) of June 7, 1993. Cf. my article "Fundamental Rights, Moral Law, and the Legal Defense of Life in a Constitutional Democracy. A Constitutionalist Approach to the Encyclical Evangelium Vitae," in *American Journal of Jurisprudence*, 43 (1998), pp. 135–183.

26. Cf. also Joseph Cardinal Ratzinger, *Wahrheit, Werte, Macht. Prüfstein der pluralistischen Gesellschaft* (Freiburg i. B.: 1993).

Human rights anchored in positive human law present just such a "counterpoint of the modern" as "a categorical legal imperative"—a condition "without whose recognition the desired pluralism is not at all viable."[27] Even leading theoreticians of pluralism speaking from outside Christianity claim that a natural law foundation for values is indispensable for a pluralistic state.[28] The "debate over the moral foundations of modern societies" is today being carried out on specifically modern premises and is fully under way in nonecclesiastical circles.[29]

A society of consistent relativists would very soon become subject to the law of the strongest. Attention to and tolerance of those who think differently, as well as true readiness for discussion and dialogue, only exists where people take convictions seriously because of their subjective conviction that their own convictions correspond to the truth. Hegel was right in saying "My conviction is of very little use, if I can't know anything as true."[30] From a relativistic point of view, one might perhaps have tolerance (that is, unconcern) toward another *opinion*; but what is needed is tolerance toward *persons* convinced of the truth of their views. Only then is a discussion meaningful. Mussolini, on the other hand, based the right of the Fascists to force others to accept their ideology specifically on the idea that there was no "objective eternal truth" and on the relativism to which that gave rise, which

---

27. Otfried Höffe, *Kategorische Rechtsprinzipien. Ein Kontrapunkt der Moderne* (Frankfurt a. M.: 1990), pp. 146–47.

28. *Ernst Fraenkel, Deutschland und die westlichen Demokratien.* Erweiterte Ausgabe, ed. by Alexander von Brünneck (Frankfurt a. M.: 1991): esp. pp. 65 ff., cf. also Joachim Detjen, *Neopluralismus und Naturrecht. Zur politischen Philosophie der Pluralismustheorie* (Paderborn: 1988). The problem is brilliantly discussed but not satisfactorily solved in Robert A. Dahl, *Democracy and its Critics* (New Haven and London: 1989).

29. A richly documented introduction to the discussions in the United States is offered by Axel Honneth, ed., *Kommunitarismus. Eine Debatte über die moralischen Grundlagen moderner Gesellschaften* (Frankfurt a. M.: 1993).

30. G. W. F. Hegel, *Grundlinien der Philosophie des Rechts [Elements of the Philosophy of Right]*, §140.

sees all ideas as equal.[31] According to this view, then, there was such a thing as relativistic fundamentalism.

Preference for peace and freedom leads the modern state to refuse to identify any particular *highest* values so as to guarantee the basic political requirements for people to live together peacefully. But the fundamentalist political fanatics are not those who believe in higher and absolute truths and try to live their lives in accord with these; they are those who believe that religious and moral highest values must be given a political grounding, since without this political-institutional enforcement and validation men could not live in peace and justice. And this is how "readiness for martyrdom is changed into readiness to kill."[32] A political ethos is converted into an ethos of salvation, ever ready to sacrifice procedural mechanisms that guarantee freedom and peace in order to achieve substantive results and impose truth, even at the cost of others' freedom.

True fundamentalism, because it is political, offers, as Manfred Spieker has so accurately pointed out, "the certainty of salvation not in heaven, but on earth. It divides the world into good and bad, friend and foe, and does not exclude the use of force from the means of gaining salvation." It is thus a threat not only to freedom but to peace.[33]

That disregard for legitimate freedom and the violation of human dignity can also occur in the name of Jesus and his Church—as to some extent appears from the motto of the Crusaders "*Deus le volt*" (God wills it)—and that people of those times who considered it necessary that heretics should

---

31. Benito Mussolini, *Diuturna*; cf. Henry B. Veatch, *Rational Man* (Bloomington and London: 1962).

32. Martin Kriele, *Einführung in die Staatslehre*, op. cit., p. 51.

33. Manfred Spieker, "Waren Petrus und Paulus, Maria und Josef Fundamentalisten? Christentum zwischen Bedrohung der Freiheit und der Suche nach Werten," in *FAZ*, no. 109, May 12, 1993, p. 12. Spieker speaks rightly about fundamentalistic tendencies in liberation theology, as seen in the work of the Boff brothers, the earlier Gustavo Gutiérrez, Hugo Assmann, et al. For the reproach of integralism in regard to liberation theology, cf. also Sutor, *Politische Ethik*, op. cit., p. 121.

die so that society might know peace were not abnormal individuals but included saints, shows how much men and institutions can be imprisoned by the prejudices of their era. Here also is the explanation for the modern fear of truth, regarded with mistrust when it concedes the rights of freedom even though the Church itself exclaims, "If you want peace, respect the conscience of every person."[34]

But isn't the Church, in proposing a new evangelization, now in the process of turning back the wheels of history? And isn't it no less a Church institution than the "powerful" and "influential" Opus Dei Prelature—among others—trying to impose upon the Church just that spirit of integralism from which it finally shook itself free at the Second Vatican Council? Aren't there just two realistic options: Either the new evangelization will *not* succeed and the whole Church will decline into a fundamentalist sect in the modern secularized world, or the new evangelization *will* succeed, which would be far worse? In what follows I can only offer my personal view, with the hope of showing that such questions about the spirit that marks Opus Dei and which it seeks to spread entirely miss the point.

OPUS DEI: LOVE FOR FREEDOM AS A CHRISTIAN PROGRAM

The central intuition of Escrivá is summed up in the statement that the heart of the Gospel, the message of Jesus, lies in "the hidden marvel of the interior life."[35] To be a Christian means following Jesus Christ closely, through the work of the Holy Spirit, in order to become one with him, so that, in the happy awareness of living as a child of God, an individual can sanctify all human activities from within, i.e., direct them through Christ to God.

---

34. John Paul II, Message on World Peace, 1991.
35. *Furrow*, no. 654.

The truth—Jesus Christ—is not spread by forcing it on others. To spread it requires that the Christian, imbedded in the structures of the world, first become fully united with God, so that he or she works as leaven in the mass.[36] In his biography of St. Josemaría, Peter Berglar reports that the founder, during the Vatican Council, replied to a bishop who enthusiastically remarked that it was the laity's task to Christianize the structures of the world: "Yes, your Excellency, but only if they have a contemplative soul. Otherwise, they will not transform anything at all; instead they will be the ones transformed. The result then will be the opposite of what you intend: instead of Christianizing the world, Christians will become worldly."[37]

What for hundreds of years seemed to demand separation from the world was suddenly seen to be the necessary elixir of life: the struggle for holiness, constant interior union with God, contemplative life, in order to infuse all human activity with the spirit of Christ's New Commandment: "By this all men will know that you are my disciples, if you have love for one another" (Jn 13:35). The *Christianization* of society means first of all living a contemplative life in order to perform "with love the most insignificant everyday action" so that it "overflows with the transcendence of God," thus making "heroic verse out of the prose of each day. Heaven and earth seem to merge, on the horizon. But where they really meet is in your hearts, when you sanctify your everyday lives."[38]

This places in sharper relief what Vatican II held to be central: "The whole Church must work vigorously in order that men may become capable of rectifying the distortion of the temporal order and directing it to God through Christ."[39]

---

36. Cf. Josemaría Escrivá, *Friends of God*, esp. "The Richness of Ordinary Life," nos. 1–22, and "Towards Holiness," nos. 294–316.

37. *Articoli del Postulatore*, 213, cited in Peter Berglar, *Josemaría Escrivá*, op. cit., p. 248.

38. Escriva, Homily "Passionately Loving the World," in *Conversations*, no. 116.

39. Decree on the apostolate of the laity, *Apostolicam Actuositatem*, no. 7.

In 1954, Escrivá formulated it like this: "Everything on earth, both material things and the temporal activities of men, needs to be directed to God (and now, after man's sin, to be redeemed and reconciled), *in accordance with the nature of each thing, and the immediate end given it by God*, but without losing sight of its supernatural final end in Jesus Christ: 'for in him all the fullness of God was pleased to dwell, and through him to reconcile to himself all things, whether on earth or in heaven, making peace by the blood of his cross' (Col 1:19–20). We must put Christ at the summit of all human activities."[40]

If these and similar formulations[41] were removed from the context of a "spirituality of leaven" rooted in interior life and contemplation, they could be wrongly interpreted and easily likened to a politico-religious program. That is true of many passages in the documents of Vatican II which speak of orienting the temporal order to Christ: only a vision of the whole enables one to understand that they are not formulating a political-religious program of an integralist character. They are too closely linked with the spirit of Christian charity and with respect for freedom for that to be the case. Confirming this spirit, Escrivá wrote a few years after the Council: "I never talk politics. I do not approve of committed Christians in the world forming a political-religious movement. That would be madness, even if it were motivated by a desire to spread the spirit of Christ in all the activities of men. What we have to do is put God in the heart of every single person, no matter who he is. . . . The kingdom of Christ is a kingdom of

---

36. Cf. Josemaría Escrivá, *Friends of God*, esp. "The Richness of Ordinary Life," nos. 1–22, and "Towards Holiness," nos. 294–316.

37. *Articoli del Postulatore*, 213, cited in Peter Berglar, *Josemaría Escrivá*, op. cit., p. 248.

38. Escriva, Homily "Passionately Loving the World," in *Conversations*, no. 116.

39. Decree on the apostolate of the laity, *Apostolicam Actuositatem*, no. 7.

40. Letter of March 19, 1954 (the italics is mine, to emphasize the autonomy of the temporal order), cited in Rodríguez, Ocáriz, Illanes, *Opus Dei in the Church*, p. 93.

41. Cf. the important homily "Christ the King" of 1970, in *Christ Is Passing By*, no. 183.

freedom. In it the only slaves are those who freely bind themselves, out of love of God."[42] As far as I can see, there is no obstacle to considering Escrivá a pioneer of love of freedom within the Church. He was a pioneer of respect for those who think differently and at the same time of the conviction—then not well-rooted and even openly rejected in ecclesiastical circles—that one could and should cooperate with everybody, reaching out above and beyond denominational or other types of barriers. He was thus the exact opposite of any typical model of integralism. [43]

To the very first members of the Work—that is, in the early 1930s—Escrivá made it plain that, while being solid in their faith, they should be upright friends of all people, so that with them they could "pull the cart in the same direction" in all possible areas and plant seeds of mutual understanding, love, forgiveness, and peace. Decades later, in a homily at an outdoor Mass on the campus of the University of Navarra, Escrivá spoke of " a Christian 'lay outlook'" that "will enable you to flee from all intolerance, from all fanaticism" and "to live in peace with all your fellow citizens, and to promote this understanding and harmony in all spheres of social life." He added: "I know I have no need to remind you of what I have been repeating for so many years. This doctrine of civic freedom, of understanding, of living together in harmony, forms a very important part of the message of Opus Dei."[44]

On the same grounds, Escrivá was concerned that—in the framework of the corporate works of Opus Dei, open to persons of all religions and faiths—no one should feel uncomfortable because of his religious convictions, and that matters of faith should not be raised with non-Catholic Christians or

---

42. Ibid., nos. 183, 184.

43. Cf. article "Integralismus" by Otto König in: *Katholisches Soziallexikon*, ed. by Alfred Klose, Wolfgang Mantl, Valentin Zsifkovits, 2nd ed. (Innsbruck: Graz, 1980): pp. 1185–1190.

44. "Passionately Loving the World," in *Conversations*, nos. 117–118.

other believers if they did not wish to discuss them. Naturally he was against any form of coercion, about which he said: "I don't understand the use of pressure either to persuade or to impose. A person who has received the faith always feels that *he* is the victor. Error is fought by prayer, by God's grace, by talking things over calmly, by study, and by getting others to study! And, above all, by charity. If anyone were to attempt to mistreat a person in error, you can be sure I would feel myself interiorly compelled to stand at his side and, for love of God, share his lot."[45]

Is not this statement in direct contradiction of the idea of "holy coercion" defended by Opus Dei's founder?[46] Aside from the fact that this phrase was very untypical of Escrivá (and as far as I know, was used only in this one place), the critics here seem to fall into a hermeneutic error,[47] besides displaying ignorance of the fact that Escrivá used the *compelle intrare* of Luke 14:23 (compel people to come in) in a way quite different from the traditional interpretation that found in it a theological justification for using force against heretics.[48]

In the parable of the wedding feast, when the master of the house finds out that some guests have declined his invitation with poor excuses, he tells his servant, "Go out into the highways and hedgerows and compel—*compelle intrare*—people to come in" (Lk 14:23). Surely this is coercion, an act of violence against the legitimate freedom of each individual conscience?

---

45. Letter of May 31, 1954, cited by Dominique Le Tourneau, *Das Opus Dei. Kurzporträt seiner Entwicklung, Spiritualität, Organisation und Tätigkeit*, 2nd ed. (Stein a. Rhein: 1988): p. 79. There is a very similar formulation in an interview with Escrivá by the French newspaper *Le Figaro*, of May 16, 1966, in *Conversations*, no. 44.

46. Cf. *The Way*, no. 387 (The first edition, under the name *Consideraciones espirituales*, was published in 1934.)

47. The Spanish original text shows more clearly than the German, that it is not a matter of using coercion for "holy" purposes, but something different from coercion, for which the word coercion is used in a metaphysical-analogical sense. Anyone who would take the expression literally would remind one of certain Pharisees in the Gospel.

48. Cf. *"Compelle Intrare," Lexikon für Theologie und Kirche*, 2nd ed., (1959), vol. 3, p. 27f.

If we meditate on the Gospel and reflect on the teachings of Jesus, we will not mistake these commands for coercion. See how gently Christ invites: "If you have a mind to be perfect . . . If any man would come after me . . . " His *compelle intrare* implies no violence, either physical or moral. Rather, it reflects the power of attraction of Christian example, which shows in its way of acting the power of God. [49]

Escrivá began to spread this spirit at a time when in Spain, and other areas, the rule in Catholic circles was a kind of integralistic triumphalism, with a general uniformity of thinking. He refused to allow Opus Dei and its members to be sucked into this current, which he viewed as a failure to accord respect to freedom. Everyone should be able to get involved wherever his Christian conscience considered right. He was opposed to any kind of "Catholic unity party," the ideal of the monolith, and apostolic exclusivism.

Escrivá had to pay dearly for this by suffering the accusation, which in its many variations has not yet disappeared, that Opus Dei was in reality a shadowy secret organization. As late as the 1960s he had to protest against pressure and slanders from the Falange.[50] Escrivá regarded freedom as a gift of God and a right of the human person, and therefore believed that a great part of the crimes committed in this world could have been avoided if mankind historically had shown greater respect for personal freedom and responsibility.

I find it hard to imagine how this view can be thought to contribute, even in tendency, to an integralistic strangling of society. To be sure, it is not a political program of any kind and therefore does not solve the problems of political culture that a Christian society would presumably have to solve. And even if this spirit of Opus Dei clearly works

49. Escrivá, Homily "Freedom, a Gift of God," in *Friends of God*, no. 37.

50. Cf. the letter of October 28, 1966 to José Solis, then head of the Falange, published in Cesare Cavalleri, *Immersed in God* (Princeton: Scepter Publishers, 1996): pp. 28–29.

against integralism,[51] that would not provide any guarantee that the new evangelization might not lead to a return to an integralist way of thinking. The fact that consciousness of this problem has not yet been well developed in the Church as a whole may account for the misunderstandings and suspicions that arise.

BEYOND INTEGRALISM: THE NEW EVANGELIZATION AND CHRISTIAN SECULARITY

According to the ideal of Opus Dei, it is the Church's task to serve as a kind of leaven encouraging people to live together harmoniously in peace, freedom, and mutual respect, being present everywhere "to eliminate hatred and cruelty, to spread throughout the earth the strong and soothing balm of love,"[52] which grows in us through personal conversion, personal inner struggle, true Christian asceticism, and the action of the spirit of God. This spirit should then be sown in every corner of society by understanding, forgiveness, service, and the personally responsible development of manifold apostolic initiatives that exclude no one from cooperation. Here is precisely that necessary openness of the Church to the world for which the last Council strove and for whose realization the Prelature of Opus Dei sees itself as a pastoral instrument in the service of the local churches.

The expression "the opening of the Church to the world" often leaves a strange clerical aftertaste. One senses an eagerness to catch up, which all too easily results in a glib secularization of the message of the salvation carried by the Church to the world. It is not bad because the world is bad, but because the real need is for that word which is not men's word

---

51. As for example in the case of the effort of some Opus Dei members to allow religious freedom and civil marriage in the then integralistic Catholic Spain. Cf. Hans Maier, "*Religionsfreiheit in den Staatlichen Verfassungen*" in the same author's *Kirche und Gesellschaft* (Munich: 1972): pp. 75–76.

52. *Christ Is Passing By*, no. 183.

but God's—a word which is drained of its power by being secularized. One "destroys the Church when one secularizes the
faith";[53] the salt that becomes insipid "will be trampled under
foot," since it is no longer of any use. For whatever a Church
"secularized" in this sense can do, modern secularized society
can do much better.

The necessary opening of the Church sought by Vatican
II is much more to be found in grasping that "the Church is
in the world through the laity."[54] But the laity bring the
Church to the world not by functioning as the long arm of the
hierarchy but simply by reason of the fact that they are baptized Christians and so called by God to the work of redemption.[55] The ordinary faithful do not live "in the Church."
They live in their families, in society, at their jobs, which only
rarely happen to be ecclesiastical ones.

Christians in today's Western world do not suffer from a
lack of pluralism or democracy. What they need is not a theology or catechesis of pluralism, but specific spiritual help
toward a lively relationship with God that empowers them to
be leaven in society and light to their fellow men and women.
It is just here that the Church becomes open to the world.
Otherwise, all it does is to open its own structures to
increased lay participation; and although that is useful and
good in many ways, it is not what really matters.

Far more decisive is that the Church go out to the world
with its own message, with every Christian feeling himself
"called by God to lead souls to sanctity. All, the great and the
small, the powerful and the weak, the wise and the simple,

---

53. Henri Cardinal du Lubac, *Zwanzig Jahre danach. Ein Gespräch über Buchstabe und Geist des Zweiten Vatikanischen Konzils* (Munich: 1985): p. 73.

54. John Paul II, Address in the Cathedral of Warsaw, June 2, 1979. Cited by Böckenförde, *"Das neue politische Engagement der Kirche. Zur 'politischen Theologie' Johannes Paulus II,"* in Böckenförde *Kirchliche Auftrag und politisches Handeln. Analyse und Orientierungen* (Schriften zu Staat-Gesellschaft-Kirche, vol. II) (Freiburg i. B.: 1989): pp. 122–145.

55. Cf. *Conversations*, nos. 21 and 112.

each in his own place, should have the humility and the great-ness to be instruments of God, to announce his kingdom. Because our Lord sent forth his followers in this way: 'Preach as you go, saying: The Kingdom of heaven is at hand'" (Mt 10:7).[56] It is necessary—even though many may think it fun-damentalism[57]—to open up this God-created world to Jesus Christ, the God who became man, without thereby destroy-ing its autonomy but in order to save it. As Kurt Koch so aptly put it, in that way the "laity's service to the world, becomes as a service to the world, a service to its salvation."[58]

The terminal point of a new evangelization is not that the world return to the past. In the logic of modern political cul-ture, the relationship between Church, state, and society will change even more.[59] But here it seems to me that an impor-tant comment is in order: The political ethos of modern times has arisen from a situation of conflict. It would be dangerous to think of the outcome of the new evangelization as being so thorough-going a Christianization as to create a conflict-free, harmonious society in which institutions for the maintenance of peace and liberty, like constitutionally anchored rights to freedom, procedural norms of justice, and formal mechanisms for resolving conflicts and protecting minorities, would be of secondary importance. I dispute this and consider it politically a very dangerous utopianism.

On the contrary, it appears to me that such institutions would be of decisive importance precisely in a "Christianized"

---

56. Josemaria Escriva, Letter of October 24, 1965 (on "Dialogue"), published in *ABC* (Madrid) May 17, 1992, p. 62f.

57. See for example the article by Peter Hebblethwaite in the magazine *Concilium*, March 1992.

58. Kurt Koch, "Christliche Sozialethik und Ekklesiologie—eine wechselseitige Herausforderung," in *Jahrbuch fur christliche Sozialwissenschaften* 32 (1989), p. 173.

59. Cf., from the viewpoint of a constitutional lawyer and historian of law, the reflec-tions by Ernst-Wolfgang Böckenförde, "*Staat-Gesellschaft-Kirche*," in the same author's *Religionsfreiheit*, op. cit., pp. 113–208; cf. also Josef Isensee, "Verfassungsrechtliche Erwartungen an die Kirche," in *Essener Gespräche zum Thema Staat und Kirche* 25 (1991), pp. 104–143.

society. They would be needed not only so that the human dignity and rights as citizens of religious and other minorities would be respected, but also so that this society of Christians would be one in which the spirit of freedom breathed. A Christian society would not be a society of saints, and exactly here is where the dangerous utopian element comes in. The Christian political ethos of freedom is not the fruit of some utopia; it is grounded in the certainty that conflict is inevitable wherever people live together. That ethos includes the ability to guarantee, to a certain point, the fundamental requirements of peace and freedom, especially through the procedural logic of institutions and without relying on individuals' ethical-religious qualities. In this way one provides institutional assurance of a minimum civilizing effect that adequately realizes the ancient dream of Aristotle and Rousseau: a government of laws. (It would take more space than is available here to develop this point as it deserves.)

Nevertheless, Catholic theology and the magisterium of the Church still oscillate between recognizing the political primacy of freedom and theologically asserting the "rights of the truth." A secular political culture is needed to establish an order of priority and a balance between these two positions. Marsilius of Padua, in the fourteenth century, was the first to recognize this problem and postulated something similar (although in a way that was not quite orthodox).

The program is therefore one of "true Christian secularity."[60] Of course, today it is still difficult for us to imagine a society that is secularized and at the same time Christian, where men live in freedom and in reciprocal respect for others, and where the Church performs its mission of helping to overcome the great obstacle to true peace among men, the sin

---

60. Martin Rhonheimer, *Natur als Grundlage der Moral. Eine Auseinandersetzung mit autonomer und teleologischer Ethik* (Innsbruck-Vienna: 1987): p. 420 [English translation: *Natural Law and Practical Reason: A Thomist View of Moral Autonomy* (New York: 2000)].

present in one's own heart—for evil proceeds from human hearts, and Christ renews hearts through the mediation of the Church. If some gods in the pantheon of modernism were then to fall from their pedestals by themselves, it would be no tragedy, since the capacity freely to make changes in its own value-framework should obviously be a basic feature of any pluralistic open society.

The existence of a political culture distinguished by respect (or, even more, love) for freedom, for peaceful coexistence, and for impartial justice, which guarantees the pluralism logically and necessarily linked to true freedom, would be a sign of the authenticity of a civilization stamped with Christian secularity. "God in creating us has run the risk and the adventure of our freedom. He wanted a history that would be a true one, the product of genuine decisions, and not one that was fiction or some sort of game. Each man has to experience his own personal autonomy with all that it implies: trial and error, guesswork and sometimes uncertainty."[61]

At the same time, this does not exclude firmness and clarity in the faith. On the contrary: if the Church, understood as the community of its faithful, wants to make Christ present in the world in freedom and with personal responsibility, thereby fulfilling its mission as a leaven in the mass, it is more than ever necessary that she and all her faithful have a clear Christian identity and fidelity in the faith. The efficacy of the Christian message does not depend simply on its truth, but "on the faithfulness and the intensity with which it is lived by the members of the Church," as E. W. Böckenförde so aptly puts it. Precisely for that reason, "it is decisively important that this message be preserved within the Church and remain alive, that it not become insipid, or be dissolved into a multiplicity. . . . The radiation of the faith can only reach the world

---

61. Josemaría Escrivá, "The Riches of the Faith," article published in the newspaper *ABC*, Madrid, November 2, 1969, reprinted in Scepter Booklet No. 5, *Life of Faith* (New York: 1974).

from the firmness and the binding content of that faith. And how can the leaven have an effect on the world, if it does not have any strength and consistency in itself?"[62] In the Church today we seem to be witnessing the spread of a hostility to so-called fundamentalism whose target is precisely clarity and firmness in the faith. Here "if holding to the truth of the faith is now 'fundamentalism,'" one might say, "then to be called 'fundamentalist' should be taken as a real compliment."[63] This empty opposition to what is mistakenly called fundamentalism, in reality based on fantastic imaginings about supposedly dangerous developments in the Church, is just what could keep the Church from fulfilling its task as leaven in the world.

Speaking to the participants in the Sixth Symposium of European bishops in 1985, John Paul II noted the emergence in the West of "a complex society, pluralistic, ambivalent," which leaves it to individuals to find "the values and the meaning of their life and actions." Modern man is alone, and "is losing hope to a terrifying degree."[64] And yet, this freedom appears to me to be an opportunity as well: for any disposition of openness to the Church and every authentic act of faith proceed from the freedom and original autonomy of man.[65] But this message requires a humble and therefore true faith on the part of the one who proclaims it. For the message to be heard, there must be new "heralds of the Gospel . . . who are experts in dealing with mankind, who thoroughly know the hearts of today's men and women, who share their joys

62. Ernst-Wolfgang Böckenförde, *Das neue politische Engagement der Kirche*, op. cit., p. 144.

63. Hans Thomas, "'Katholischer Fundamentalismus'. Zum Mechanismus einer akademischen Debatte," *Forum Katholische Theologie*, 8:4 (1992), pp. 260–277.

64. *Die europäischen Bischöfe und die Neu-Evangelisierung Europas*, published by the Secretariat of the German Bishops Conference and the CCEE Secretariat St. Gallen (*Stimmen der Weltkirche Europas* 32), October 1991, p. 243.

65. Cf. Martin Rhonheimer, "L'uomo, un progetto di Dio. La fondazione teonomica dell'autonomia morale secondo L'Enciclica Veritatis Splendor," in *L'Osservatore Roman*, 5, (Sept. 6, 1993), pp. 1 and 4.

and hopes, fears and sorrows and at the same time want to be contemplative friends of God. This also requires new saints."[66]

One thing more appears to me necessary as a prerequisite. In the words of Escrivá: "The principal apostolate we Christians must carry out in the world, and the best witness we can give of our faith, is to help bring about a climate of genuine charity within the Church. For who indeed could feel attracted to the Gospel if those who say they preach the Good News do not really love one another, but spend their time attacking one another, spreading slander, and quarrelling?"[67]

---

66. John Paul II, Address on October 11, 1985 at the Sixth Symposium of European Bishops, in *Die europäischen Bischöfe und die Neuevangelisierung Europas*, op. cit., p. 244. Cf. letter on "The New Evangelization" by Bishop Alvaro del Portillo (Prelate of Opus Dei) to the faithful of the Prelature, December 25, 1985, in *Romana: Bolletino della Prelatura della Santa Croce e Opus Dei*, II (1986), pp. 79–84.

67. Josemaría Escrivá, *Friends of God*, no. 226.

CHAPTER 4

Truth and Politics
in Christian Society

JOSEMARÍA ESCRIVÁ AND LOVE FOR FREEDOM:
PRESENTED IN A HISTORICAL-THEOLOGICAL PERSPECTIVE

I. A stroll through history. The connection between truth and justice in regard to religious freedom and its solution through the Second Vatican Council

THE BEGINNINGS: THE ROMAN EMPIRE, CHRISTIANITY, AND FREEDOM OF THE CHURCH

Uno itinere non potest perveniri ad tam grande secretum: "It is not possible to reach a mystery so exalted [as that of God] by a single path." With these words, pronounced in his famous *relatio* of the year 384 to the Christian emperor Valentinian II, the Roman senator Symmachus, head of the pagan minority in a society that had converted to Christianity, opposed the Gospel affirmation: "I am the way, and the truth, and the life; no one comes to the Father, but by me" (Jn 14:6). Symmachus's view was that the mystery of God was manifested in various ways over the course of history—in other words, all religions had their share of the truth. *Quid interest, qua quisque prudentia verum requirat?* "What difference does it make from what viewpoint someone seeks truth? Don't we all look at the same stars, dwell under the same heaven, live in the same world?"[1]

As we know, the attempt by Symmachus to revive the traditional religious pluralism of pagan Rome was unsuccessful. The Christians did not consider the pagan gods other manifestations of the divinity, but demons whose cult had to be eradicated from human society. Traditional Roman pluralism, with pagan divinities permeating all expressions of political and social life, could be tolerant only toward religions that made no claim to universal truth. But Judaeo-Christian monotheism was incompatible with the Roman *pantheon* that was part of the ideology of the Empire. After the Constantinian about-face, toleration of the Christian religion began. Later it acquired a privileged position, while the pagan cults were merely tolerated; and finally Christianity, which had become the religion of the majority (and particularly the emperors), became more and more intolerant. It prohibited all pagan worship, destroyed the temples and statues of the gods, expropriated their sacred lands, condemned various books to the fire, and finally was elevated to the rank of religion of the Empire under Emperor Theodosius, a contemporary of St. Ambrose of Milan.

Christianity's growing intolerance and hostility toward paganism were justified as a defense against its earlier persecutors and because of fear of a possible reversal of the situation. But to understand this evolution deeply one must interpret it also as a process by which the Christian religion took the place of the old, highly polytheistic imperial religion.

The first members of Christian society were Romans, and the members continued to be such. The words *in hoc signo vinces* (in this sign you will conquer), seen by Constantine before his decisive battle at the Milvian Bridge, were for him

---

1. "*Q. Aurelii Symmachi quae supersunt*," Otto Seeck, ed., (*Monumenta Germaniae historica, Auctores antiquissimi VI, I*) (Berlin: Weidmannsche Verlagsbuchhandlung, 1883, reprinted 1961): p. 282.

a promise that the God of the Christians would bring victory over his adversaries to him and greatness and stability to Rome. The key to understanding the intimate union between Imperial Rome and Christianity, as well as the subsequent intolerance of Christianized Rome toward pagans, Christian heretics, and to some extent Jews, was not only fear of a possible relapse into paganism, but also the typically Roman idea that the worship of the true God would guarantee the Empire's greatness and welfare.

There was no lack of attempts, especially under Emperor Constantius, to control the Church, to the point of bringing it under the power of the state. Thus began the struggle for the *libertas ecclesiae*, the freedom of the Church, which saw itself obliged to defend its independence in the face of the meddling of the temporal power. At the same time, both the Church and its faithful became true patriots of the Roman Empire, since they considered themselves responsible for its greatness and happiness.

Rome's traumatic conquest and sacking in 410 by a high officer of the Roman army, the Goth Alaric, allowed people to denounce the Christian religion as the cause of that humiliating and unprecedented calamity: the cause of Rome's fall was ascribed to unfaithfulness to the old Roman gods.[2] In this precarious situation it was St. Augustine who finally severed the dangerous connection between the Roman Empire and the Christian religion with his work *De Civitate Dei*. It marked an epochal change. The worship of the true God, St. Augustine affirmed, did not aim to make Rome great or to maintain its power and splendor, but to lead mankind to its heavenly dwelling place.

The great Bishop of Hippo, a true Roman patriot, thus gave classic expression to what is called Christian dualism.

---

2. Cf. Pierre Chuvin, *Chronique des derniers païens. La disparition du paganisme dans l'Empire romain, du règne de Constantin à celui de Justinien* (Paris: Les Belles Lettres/Fayard, 1990): p. 86ff.

According to the distinctions of Augustine, the unity between Empire and Church was broken into two parts: an earthly part, which seeks the "conservation of mortal life" and has as its task to subject men to a system of peace and common life, legitimate as long as it poses no obstacle to religion, which teaches the worship of the true God; and a heavenly part, the Kingdom of God, which becomes a reality in the hearts of men.[3]

Unfortunately, the intransigence, fanaticism, and schemes of the Donatists finally led even St. Augustine, who had always opposed using the coercive power of the state against heretics and had instead defended the power of the word and of dialogue, to support the use of state power. Thus, for the first time, he used the *compelle intrare* of the Gospel (cf. Lk 14:23) as theological justification for the use of the coercive power of the temporal authority to force men to abandon the way of heresy and return to Christian truth.[4] Note, though, that if St. Augustine opted for the use of state power, it was above all due to the fact that the Donatists themselves used violence to impose their beliefs on Catholics where they held power. "Why then should not the Church use force to bring back to her bosom the children who have gone astray, since those same lost children have used force to send others to perdition."[5]

POLITICAL-RELIGIOUS UNITY: THE MEDIEVAL *RESPUBLICA CHRISTIANA* AND THE CAUSES OF ITS COLLAPSE

In the century that followed Constantine's conversion, what could be understood as self-defense by the Church against the threat of a return of persecution and the earlier paganism, and what in St. Augustine was a response to an especially complex

---

3. Cf. Augustine, *De Civitate Dei*, XIX, 17.

4. St. Augustine, *Contra Gaudentium*, I, XXV, 28 (CSEL 53, 226f); Epist. 93 and 185.

5. St. Augustine, Epist. 185, 6, 23: "*Cur ergo non cogeret Ecclesia perditos filios ut redirent, si perditi filii coegerunt alios ut perirent?*" PL 33, 803.

situation, soon became a more and more commonly accepted principle: namely, that the secular arm of the state should be at the service of the Church and its truth. Pope Gregory the Great, a holy man of prayer and spirituality, went beyond the Augustinian idea that the temporal power should *limit itself to not hindering* the worship of the true God and affirmed in his letters that "the earthly realm should be at the service of the heavenly realm."[6] The celebrated formula of Pope Gelasius, who distinguished the *power* of kings and the sacred *authority* of the popes, thus paved the way to viewing the power of princes as something needed, as St. Isidore of Seville put it, to impose "with the terror of the discipline what the clergy was not able to bring about with words alone."[7]

The first consequence of this new reading, undoubtedly mistaken, of Augustinian dualism[8] was the consecration of the temporal power. With the rebirth under Charlemagne of the Roman Empire (later known as the empire "of the Germans"), the emperors assumed an ecclesiastical-sacred mission at the service of the spiritual and supernatural goals of the Church. The result was an integration of the Church's spiritual authority into temporal power structures, to the extent that the bishops became political pillars of the Empire.

Eventually, the terms were altered in the investiture conflicts—the second great battle for ecclesial freedom—and the Church freed itself from this linkage with temporal structures that endangered the carrying out of its spiritual mission. Making use of Roman law, especially the ancient *lex regia*, and considering themselves as the true heirs of the Roman Empire, the popes of the High Middle Ages not only attributed to themselves the highest *auctoritas* in the spiritual sense,

---

6. St. Gregory the Great, *Epistle 3*, 65.

7. Sententiae, Bk 3, ch. 51 (P.L. 83, 723–724; the Latin text of this passage is found in Henri Xavier Arquillière, *L'Augustinism politique. Essai sur la formacion des theories politiques du Moyen-Age* (Paris: J. Vrin, 1955): p. 142.

8. Cf. Henri-Xavier. Arquillière, op. cit.: *Jean-Jacques Chevalier, Storia del pensiero politico*, Vol I, 2nd ed. (Bologna: 1989): p. 256ff.

but also the *plenitudo potestatis*, the fullness of power: their motives were certainly pastoral, but the results had an inescapably political dimension.

Such a plenitude of power permitted the popes to exercise an effective and direct jurisdiction, *ratione peccati* (for reasons of sin), as it was then called, over temporal princes. This is to say that the pope exercised an effective power for pastoral reasons, which were always difficult to distinguish clearly from political ones: a sinning prince could be deposed by the pope, especially if he was seen as posing a threat to the eternal salvation of his subjects. In this period, as a result of the doctrine of the "two swords," only the Roman Pontiff could claim true sovereignty for himself. He considered himself the supreme feudal lord and all Christian princes his vassals.[9]

This medieval *Respublica Christiana* constituted a religious-political unity in which the spiritual supremacy of the Church was intertwined with the temporal feudal order. The Catholic faith was a condition of citizenship. Heresy was considered an injury to the temporal common good, besides being a crime of *lèse majesté* punishable by death.[10] But this unity shattered due to two developments of decisive importance: the emergence of territorial states with their respective sovereigns, and the fragmenting of the unity of faith as a result of the Protestant Reformation.

The wars of religion, provoked by the tenacious conviction that unity between the public political order and Christian orthodoxy was necessary, led to a formula of provisional peace that proved decisive: *cuius regio, eius religio*—the religion of a state was to be whatever its territorial sovereign

---

9. Further details, a bibliography, and sources can be found in: Rhonheimer, *Perché una filosofia politica?* op. cit.

10. The norm contained in the [twelfth century] *Decretum Gratianum* (38, 23, 4) according to which "*haeretici ad salutem etiam inviti sunt trahendi*" went far beyond Augustine's *cogite intrare*, precisely because it presupposed medieval religious-political unity. Although St. Augustine opted for "political" measures against heretics, he did not speak of using penal law, and he was never in favor of the death penalty for heretics.

determined.[11] The result was religious intolerance, together with a fatal symbiosis between the Church and the absolutist state. In Catholic countries (especially France and Austria) and even more in the Papal States, the temporal power considered itself the protector of Catholic truth and the Church an aid to the good functioning of the absolutist state. This arrangement, nevertheless, began to lose its legitimacy because of economic and social factors and the emergence of the liberal-constitutional movement. In opposition to the uncontrolled and arbitrary power of the absolute state and a Church that was privileged and rich (in France, the Church before the Revolution possessed some ten percent of all of the national territory), and in opposition to a society permeated with clericalism, the liberal movement demanded civil liberties and the submission of power to law, together with the Church's renunciation of its privileged position.

CONFRONTATION AND MISUNDERSTANDINGS: THE CATHOLIC CHURCH, THE MODERN WORLD, AND THE WEIGHT OF A MORE THAN THOUSAND-YEAR-OLD TRADITION

A tortuous process ensued, violent and revolutionary in part, in which legitimate claims mingled with exaggerations, excesses, and fanaticisms. It is not necessary to review this history now.[12] The attempt in the nineteenth century to restore the old order and the struggle against it on the part of the liberal movement were often accomplished by a growing anticlericalism where fanaticism and violence even went so far as the laicist attempt to deny the Catholic Church any

---

11. For an understanding of the process that led to that solution, see the classic study by Joseph Lecler, *Histoire de la tolerance au siècle de la Réforme* (1955) (Paris: 1994).

12. See, for example, Giacomo Martina, *Storia della Chiesa da Lutero ai nostri giorni, vol. 3: L'età de liberalismo* (Brescia: Morcelliana, 1995); Cesare Marongiu Buonaiuti, *Chiesa e Stati. Dall'età dell'Illuminismo alla Prima guerra mondiale* (Rome: La Nova Italia Scientifica, 1994); Guido de Ruggiero, *Historia del Liberalismo Europeo* (1925) (Rome-Bari: Laterza, 1984).

civil status and public influence as a visible and legally organized organism. In this way the nineteenth-century popes
were pushed toward making common cause with people who
saw in modern freedoms no more than a threat to the social
order, a menace to the stability of governments, and a falling
away from the true faith.

The weight of centuries of history and the conviction, a
tradition by now, that it was up to the temporal power to preserve the true religion and the worship of the true God in
society, led the popes of that century to see in modern freedoms, particularly "freedom of conscience" and "freedom of
religion," an invitation to religious indifference and arbitrary
freedom: that is, freedom in regard to the truth. Since political liberalism at times joined relativistic and agnostic ideas to
its demands for freedom, the Church identified modern freedoms (especially religious freedom) with the assertion that
there was no one truth in religious matters and that individual consciences had no obligation to seek such a truth and
embrace it once known.

Freedom of religion and of conscience, therefore, were
condemned together, as being equivalent to a denial of the
dominion of truth and God over man—as well as a denial of
the obligation of the temporal power to protect and support
the Catholic Church as the only *true* religion. Only the
truth—not error—had a right to exist, the pontiffs argued. To
affirm the existence of a right to religious freedom would in
effect have meant affirming that error has a right to exist in
society. No, said the popes: error, like much else, can be tolerated by the sovereign power if it sees such a need, but only
for the sake of safeguarding a higher good.

Thus, Pius IX confirmed in *Quanta Cura* the condemnation issued by Gregory XVI of freedom of conscience and of
religion, understood as a "right proper to each person that
should be proclaimed by law." And while condemning the
opposite opinion, he defended the duty of the state to
"repress with the established penalties the transgressors of

the Catholic religion," not only when this was required for public peace, but precisely because it was required by the truth of the Catholic religion and its consequent right to be supported and fostered for the good of men and society.[13] In substance, this was the doctrine of the Catholic Church from Leo XIII[14] to Pius XII, although its form was gradually mitigated and modified by the making of distinctions as the position of the Church on this question grew increasingly anachronistic in a society that was becoming more and more secularized and pluralistic.[15]

It will be obvious that in this presentation I have limited myself to synthesizing a doctrinal position in its relation to the history of ideas and have done so at the level of conceptual abstraction. It is impossible to do justice here either to the

---

13. Cf. *Enchiridion delle encicliche 2: Gregory XVI, Pius I* (Bologna: 1996): p. 505 (no. 319). "Freedom of conscience" was widely used in the eighteenth and nineteenth centuries as a synonym for "freedom of worship" or "freedom of religion": the civil right of individuals to accept and practice the religion they consider right, unhampered by the state or any other public authority. But it was also used alone to signify a subjectivistic free-thinking approach allied to relativism and agnosticism. Unfortunately, the two meanings were not always sufficiently distinguished.

14. Cf. his encyclical *Libertas* of June 20 1888, in: *Enchiridion delle encicliche 3: Leo XIII* (Bologna: 1997): p. 469 ff (no. 652 ff.)

15. Cf. Pius XII, Address *Ci Riesce*, of December 6, 1953, *AAS* 45 (1953), pp. 794–802. Some authors try to see in *Ci Riesce* the doctrine of a "right of tolerance," for instance, Fr. Basile (Valuet), *La Liberté religieuse et la tradition catholique. Un cas de développement doctrinal homogène dans le magistère authentique*, Abbaye Sainte Madeleine du Barroux, 1998, vol. 1,1, pp. 187–221 (a rich and well-intentioned work, although erroneous in my judgment from the methodological point of view as well as in its conclusions). According to Fr. Basile, the doctrine of *Ci Riesce* affirms a "right of tolerance" and foreshadows the doctrine of Vatican II on the "right to religious freedom." This does not seem correct to me, because the teaching of *Ci Riesce* in principle does not provide a rule of conduct that is to extend over a specific sphere of activity, namely, the religious, but merely applies, as Pius XII stresses in his talk, to "particular circumstances" according to the judgment of the "Catholic statesman," and only after the judgment of the Church has been heard. One cannot derive a "right" to anything from this. The arguments that Fr. Basile uses to overcome this difficulty (ibid., pp. 217 ff) make the very text of *Ci Riesce* and its simple and clear teaching irrelevant and substitute a series of arguments lacking in coherence. What this point of view overlooks is that *Ci Riesce* continues to imply a vision in which the sovereignty of the state is not *essentially limited by determined personal rights*, such as that of religious freedom. On the contrary, the vision of Pius XII is that of a state that in the exercise of its discretionary power can tolerate what it judges to be an evil in order to avoid a greater evil or attain a more important good.

highly nuanced and flexible way in which the popes mentioned and the Church as a whole actually conducted themselves, or to the pastoral impact of the popes' pronouncements, or to the great complexity and ambiguity of the historical situation.[16]

It is no less necessary to emphasize that until Pius IX, the popes, besides being pastors, were temporal rulers, who exercised the power of a secular prince within the Papal States, with an army, police, and censorship. They could enforce the norms of canon law by force of arms and deny the rights of citizenship to those who did not profess the Catholic religion. Not that they wanted to exercise temporal power—they simply were convinced that only in that way could they safeguard the Church's independence and freedom against the powers of this world. This partly explains the hostility of the Church in the nineteenth century to modernity. The struggle of the pontiffs against "modern freedoms" combined a necessary and justified vigilance over the essential principles of Catholic doctrine with a concrete interest in maintaining the internal order of their state and assuring its temporal sovereignty against constitutional, liberal, nationalist, and therefore revolutionary demands.[17]

In the concrete circumstances of that time, it was not always easy to see that the position of the popes, just described,

---

16. This ambiguity can be seen in the fact that at the end of the nineteenth century, liberalism, particularly in Italy, ended up by being an oppressor of freedom. The liberal Guido de Ruggiero, in his famous *Historia del Liberalismo Europeo* (cited above), which appeared in 1925, denounced the "dogmatic absolutism" of a certain kind of liberalism which tried to "deny to the Church the right of being a free citizen in the state" (p. 425), "converting liberalism itself into a dogma no less intolerable and oppressive" (p. 428), in such a way that he could conclude that "the resistance of the Church against the state 'tyranny,' although its interior motive had nothing to do with liberalism, represented in fact an exercise and a defense of freedom" (p. 429).

17. Cf. the very useful *Storia della Chiesa*, of Augustine Fliche and Victor Martin (in 24 vol.); vol. 20: *Restaurazione e crisi liberale 1815–1846* of Roger Aubert (Milan: Edizione Paoline, 1990). A different view is provided by Roberto De Mattei, *Pius IX* (Casale Monferrato: Edizione Piemme, 2000): this is a well-documented apologia for the viewpoint of the Church in the nineteenth century, and which apparently does not fully accept the teaching of the Second Vatican Council in regard to religious freedom (cf. note 58 on p. 185).

with regard to the relationship between religious truth and the rights and duties of the temporal power derived from teachings of very different weights. On the one hand, some of the principles are properly essential to the Church of Christ, such as the doctrine of the oneness and truth of the Catholic Church, willed by God and invested with a divine redemptive mission in regard to the whole human race; the doctrine that the temporal power is obliged to respect this mission and the Church's indispensable freedom, in the sense of creating conditions favorable for it to fulfill its task in addition to not obstructing it; or, finally, the doctrine of each person's obligation in the matter of religion to seek the truth and embrace it when it is known. These Catholic doctrines, part of the deposit of faith, were mixed together with the idea—which to a certain extent goes back to the Roman conception of the unity of the Empire and the worship of the true God—that the powers of this world—the state and, with it, the institutions of society— are obliged to recognize the Church's freedom precisely because of their recognition of its truth and unicity, so that where the Church demands a *right*, they can concede to the other religions at most a precarious *tolerance*.[18]

---

18. This makes it clear that, as we shall see, the change effected by the Second Vatican Council is not a matter of *Catholic doctrine*, but rather of certain conceptions about the role of society and the temporal power in relation to religious truth and, consequently, to the Church. Therefore, it is a matter of a change at the level of the Church's social teaching. For the same reason, the partial rupture at this level of continuity between the teaching of Vatican II and "traditional" teaching does not call into question the infallibility of the ordinary universal magisterium (cf. Vatican II, *Lumen Gentium*, 25, *Enchiridion Vaticanum I*, 173 ff. [no. 3 ff.]). The thesis of partial continuity that I am trying to maintain in these pages was proposed very clearly by Ernst-Wolfgang Böckenförde, *Religionsfreiheit*, op. cit. Partial continuity also was maintained in another way, in the sense that there was no substantial opposition between Vatican II and the preceding magisterium, despite the fact that there was an authentic novelty in the Council's teachings. Cf. for example Fernando Ocáriz, "*Sulla libertà religiosa, Continuità del Vaticano II con il Magistero precedente,*" in *Annales Theologici 3* (1989): pp. 71–97 (although the author's argument is not completely convincing to me). As for the thesis entirely opposed to mine—i.e., total continuity and homogeneity between Vatican II and the earlier position—which was most notably argued by Bertrand de Margerie, *Liberté religiouse et règne du Christ* (Paris: Édition du Cerf, 1988), and afterward in his monumental work (cf. above, note 15) by Fr. Basile [Valuet]—its principal argument is based on the fact that Popes Pius VI, Gregory

So the problem comes down to this: For someone who argues that the obligation of the public authority of the state to recognize the freedom of the Catholic Church is rooted in its being the only *true* Church and religion, there can be no right to religious freedom for others besides Catholics. And in that case it would be inconceivable that a secular state declare itself incompetent in religious matters and allow freedom to all beliefs and religious communities—to be sure, always with

---

XVI, and Pius IX did not condemn freedom of the press, religious freedom, and freedom of worship, etc., *as such*, but only as found in an *unlimited* (that is to say, absolute) and therefore excessive form (Bertrand de Margerie, op. cit., pp. 20 ff.), a critique which remains valid today. Taking the historical context as a whole, this thesis—as well as the general view of these authors—seems to me to be difficult to sustain: in the first place, it seems to overlook the fact that Pius VI (cf. Brief *Quod Aliquantum* of 1791, in which he condemned the French Revolution's Declaration of the Rights of Man and of the Citizen) saw the error of modern freedoms as residing essentially in the fact that in claiming them, *Catholics* attributed to themselves freedoms outside of the control of the Church (thus Pius VI saw no problem for "infidels and Jews," who "should not be obliged to the obedience prescribed for Catholics"; cited by Fr. Basile, op. cit., vol. 2, p. 1035). For Pius VI, the problem of modern freedoms was that precisely as *civil liberties* they were seen as contrary to the due submission of the Catholic faithful to the Church. In the second place, the thesis of total continuity does not seem to take sufficiently into consideration the fact that for Gregory XVI "unlimited" (immoderate) and "unrestrained" freedom of opinion, of the press, etc., necessarily had to mean a liberty not "controlled" or "moderated" by state censorship. His concern, in other words, was with the liberal demand for the abolition of state censorship, of the more or less arbitrary and uncontrollable exercise of state power, and of the inquisition of the Holy Office, in reference to the press (which did not mean absolute freedom, since liberals such as Benjamin Constant opted for restrictions and regulations based on laws; what they opposed was the arbitrariness of the censors, while they supported procedures typical of a state governed by law). Therefore, what was being condemned was more a particular political conception, that is, a specific conception of the state and its functions. The condemnation was mingled in an inappropriate way with the condemnation of religious indifferentism. This happened because it was thought the Church essentially required a secular arm or, what was the same, that the temporal power was at the service of the Catholic Church for the dissemination of Christian truth in society. The discontinuity between the position of these popes and the doctrine of Vatican II was precisely at this political-juridical level. It left untouched the proper content of Catholic doctrine that formed part of the deposit of the faith, as for example, the submission of conscience to the truth and the duty of every man to seek religious truth.

(For this see the address to the Roman Curia on December 22, 2005 by Pope Benedict XVI, where he refers to the Church's doctrine on religious liberty, distinguishing between the continuity of principles and the discontinuity of historical application of these principles. This corresponds exactly to my thesis of "partial discontinuity" in the Church's teaching on religious liberty.

the qualification that public order, defined by law according to impartial rules, is not injured.

THE SECOND VATICAN COUNCIL: DISSOLUTION OF THE JURIDICAL-POLITICAL UNITY BETWEEN TRUTH AND RELIGIOUS FREEDOM

It was the Second Vatican Council that opened a new path and dissolved the connection between the Catholic religion's claim to possess the truth and its demand for state recognition of its freedom. True, in the "Declaration on Religious Freedom" *Dignitatis Humanae* (DH),[19] the Council affirmed that it left "intact the traditional Catholic teaching on the moral duty of individuals and societies toward the true religion and the one Church of Christ."[20] But in the context of conciliar teaching this doctrine was "cleansed" of certain elements of a nonessential character.

There has been considerable discussion of that assertion, which is situated at the beginning of the conciliar declaration. The *Catechism of the Catholic Church*, a mature fruit of Vatican II, seems to have closed this discussion by proposing its authentic interpretation. As far as individual persons are concerned, the Catechism understands the "traditional Catholic teaching" as concerning simply a "duty of offering God genuine worship."[21] In contrast, the "duty of societies" is twofold: there is the Church's duty—to evangelize mankind and thus "to infuse the Christian spirit into the mentality and mores, laws and structures of the communities in which [its members]

---

19. The English translation used here is that of *Vatican Council II: The Conciliar and Post Conciliar Documents* edited by Austin Flannery, O.P. (Northport, NY: Costello Publishing Co., 1987).

20. DH, 1 (1044). The numbers in parenthesis are the marginal numbers of *Enchiridion Vaticanum I: Documenti del Concilio Vaticano II*, relating to *Dignitatis Humanae* (cited as DH).

21. *Catechism of the Catholic Church* (CCC) 2105. This should be read in the light of the preceding paragraph (2104) of the Catechism.

live";[22] and there is a "social duty of Christians"— "to respect and awaken in each man the love of the true and the good. It requires them to make known the worship of the one true religion which subsists in the Catholic and apostolic Church. Christians are called to be the light of the world."[23] In other words, for the *Catechism of the Catholic Church* the "traditional Catholic teaching on the moral duty of individuals and societies toward the true religion and the one Church of Christ," which, in line with the intention of the Council, remains intact, includes the duty all have to seek the truth, especially in what refers to God and to his Church[24] (as we shall see, this is a fundamental principle of *Dignitatis Humanae*), the duty of the Church to evangelize, and the duty of Catholics to help others know the truth of the Catholic religion by means of their apostolate.

In this way, any kind of indifferentism, which in the past was associated with the idea of religious freedom, is rejected. What this "traditional Catholic doctrine" does *not* appear to imply, however, is any duty on the part of the state to give public recognition to the truth of the Church of Christ and to guarantee society's permeation with the salvific message of Christ (a duty whose denial meant religious indifferentism to the popes of the nineteenth century).[25] This passage of the Catechism concludes with these words: "Thus the Church shows forth the kingship of Christ over all creation and in particular over human societies."[26] Thus it is not the state's mission to manifest that reign over society, since that is the

---

22. Ibid. (The Catechism here quotes *Apostolicam Actuositatem*, no. 13.)

23. Ibid. (This quote is from DH, no. 1.)

24. CCC, 2104.

25. Anyone interested in understanding the extent to which this doctrine was present up till a few years before the Council might profitably read the article by Antonio Messineo, "Laicismo politica e dottrina cattolica," in *La Civiltà Cattolica*, 103 (1952), vol. 2, pp. 18–28; cf. also Alfredo Ottaviani, op. cit., Univ. Lateranense (Vatican City: Typ. Polygl. Vaticanis, 1960): pp. 46–77.

26. CCC, 2105.

evangelizing mission of the Church and the apostolate of the Catholic faithful in society.

With regard to what concerns its essential doctrinal content, Catholic tradition is thus fully confirmed. Not all religions have the same value. There exists a single religious truth, of which the Catholic Church is the depository and which should be sought by every person. In addition, the Church is the instrument by which the realm and spirit of Christ inform all created realities and, in particular, human society. But it was necessary to abandon, as not part of traditional Catholic doctrine and the deposit of faith, the idea of the temporal power as "the secular arm" of the Church for the fulfillment of that mission and the demand to receive explicit recognition of its unicity and truth, carrying with it a privileged juridical-political position for the Catholic Church.

This does not mean that, as Vatican II sees it, the state no longer has any duties toward the Church and the Catholic religion. Quite the contrary. But Vatican II no longer bases this duty on the idea that the Church is the depository of the only *true* religion, endowed with a divine mission, but rather on the right to religious freedom possessed by all men and creeds. This right—which is essentially protection against any coercion exercised by individuals, social groups, and any human powers, and which therefore possesses the character of a civil right—consists in the double freedom enjoyed by every person: first, not to be forced to act contrary to his or her conscience and, second, not to be impeded, individually or corporately, in acting according to conscience.[27] Ultimately, the right of religious freedom is based on the human person's dignity as a spiritual being, free and responsible, created in the image of God, with a corresponding obligation to seek the truth and adhere to it when known.[28]

---

27. DH 2 and 3 (1045 and 1049).

28. DH 2 (1045); 3 (1047 ff).

This right to religious freedom in its double aspect—above all, the ability to follow one's own conscience in religious matters, valid for all men and beliefs—the Church now claims for itself. The temporal power, the Council argues, is incompetent in religious matters, for a simple reason: religious acts "transcend by their very nature the earthly and temporal order," so that the state should "recognize and look with favor on the religious life of the citizens" without trying to "control or restrict religious activity."[29] The secular state is not a "laicist" state in the sense of being agnostic and denying the capital importance of the religious phenomenon or the possible existence of truth in this field. Nor does it desire to exclude religion and its corporate expressions from public life. But the temporal power is blind and impartial from the denominational point of view; and, within the limits imposed by respect for the imperatives of public order, it recognizes full freedom.[30]

FREEDOM OF THE CHURCH AND RELIGIOUS FREEDOM: IMPLICATIONS OF A TEACHING

Dignitatis Humanae,13 is of capital importance for the new understanding of the *libertas ecclesiae* and of the duties of state power in relation to the Church. In the first of its three paragraphs it affirms that it is necessary "that the Church enjoy that freedom of action which her responsibility for the salvation of men requires." Those who attack this sacred freedom of the Church of Jesus Christ "oppose the will of God." This implies that because of its faith the Church has the duty to defend its freedom. Freedom is therefore "the fundamental principle governing relations between the Church and public authorities and the whole civil order."[31]

---

29. DH 3 (1051).

30. On the concept of public order (as distinct from the common good) a useful source is Avelino Manuel Quintas, *Analisi del bene commune* (Rome: Bulzone Editore, 1988).

31. DH 13 (1075).

It must be emphasized that this is said *from the point of view of the Catholic Church itself,* that is to say, *sub luce revelationis* (in the light of Revelation).[32] And for just that reason, this point of view need *not* be recognized by the public powers; in fact, such recognition would contradict what was said in the first part of the conciliar declaration about the state's lack of competence in this area. What DH 13 presents is the Church's self-understanding or consciousness of itself, according to which opposing its salvific mission would be opposing the will of God. This consciousness of itself grounds the Church's grave obligation to fight for its freedom, as well as its insistence that this freedom be fully recognized.

On the basis of what is said in the first paragraph, the second paragraph of DH 13 explains that the Church claims in regard to the civil powers "freedom as a spiritual authority, appointed by Christ the Lord with the duty, imposed by divine command, of going into the whole world and preaching the Gospel to every creature." Clearly, for the Church the basis for asking and applying to itself the right to religious freedom is supernatural faith in its mission. The right is applied to the Church insofar as it is an *institution with a specific pastoral mission* ("as a spiritual authority"). And the same paragraph adds a second aspect: the Church claims this freedom also because it is a society of men, each of whom as an individual has "the right to live in civil society in accordance with the demands of the Christian faith."[33]

Finally, the third paragraph relates what has just been said to the doctrine on religious freedom expressed in the first part of the conciliar text: if a country's practice and legal order respect the principle of religious freedom, "then does the Church enjoy in law and in fact those stable conditions which

---

32. This is how the title of the second part of *Dignitatis Humanae* expresses it. While in the first part the doctrine of religious freedom is proposed in its "general aspects," in the second part it is explained "in the light of revelation."

33. DH 13 (1076).

give her the independence necessary for fulfilling her divine mission. Ecclesiastical authorities have been insistent in claiming this independence in society."[34] This is the first point: by means of the "principle of religious freedom" the Church is satisfactorily granted that freedom which in past centuries she demanded not only by reason of her awareness of being entrusted with a divinely given mission but also in virtue of her claim to be the only such religious body and therefore deserving of public recognition as the only *true* religion. Now, however, the Council has determined that public recognition of the right to religious freedom, a right enjoyed by all religions within the bounds of public order, is sufficient to ensure the *libertas ecclesiae*.

The Council's text adds still another aspect: the Church not only can realize its mission as an *institution* on the basis of the "principle of religious freedom," but "at the same time the Christian faithful, *in common with the rest of men*, have the civil right of freedom from interference in leading their lives according to their conscience."[35] The text concludes with the affirmation that, in consequence, "a harmony exists therefore between the freedom of the Church and that religious freedom which must be recognized as the right of all men and all communities and must be sanctioned by constitutional law."[36]

For the first time since the elevation of Christianity to the position of official religion of the Roman Empire, the Catholic Church has set itself on an equal plane with other religions in what concerns the civil order and political exigencies, without asking privileges of any kind based on its claim to be the *true* religion.

The Church has also abandoned in its social doctrine the principle that only truth, and not error, has rights. It is not that the human conscience no longer is obliged to seek the

---

34. DH 13 (1077).

35. Ibid. (the italics are mine).

36. Ibid.

truth and adhere to it once found; but now nothing is said about the distinction between truth and error as a rule for delineating relations between persons, citizens, and the public authority. In accord with the teaching of Vatican II, at the level of the juridical-political order, in religious matters it is not any longer the *truth* which primarily counts, but the rights of *persons* as free and responsible beings. What matters, too, is the ability of religious communities, among them the Catholic Church, to develop their mission in full freedom, including being able to count on—insofar as it is consistent and compatible with the secular principles of a state governed by law—support from the public authority.

It is true that the teaching of the Church has always recognized everyone's right not to be compelled to embrace the Christian religion against his own will or conscience, and this was emphasized by the Council.[37] But now this freedom is completed by a new affirmation of the right all people have to be able to follow their own consciences in religious matters, both individually and corporately, without being impeded by any person, social group, or human power.

According to the traditional doctrine, although a Muslim or a Jew had a right not to be forced to embrace the Christian faith, he did not have the right to live without discrimination in civil society as Muslim or Hebrew. The Muslim and the Jew could only be *tolerated* at the discretion of the sovereign. This traditional doctrine was fully compatible with the practice followed in the past by some Catholic countries of expelling Jews who did not want to embrace the Christian faith or shutting them up in a ghetto, denying them civil rights and the exercise of most professions and trades, as well as ownership of land and real estate.

The expansion of view introduced by Vatican II implied a change of vision regarding the relationship between the

---

37. DH 12 (1073).

Catholic Church and society. This was apparent above all in its social doctrine. The Church seemed to recall once more the wisdom of St. Augustine, who asked of the temporal power only that it not place obstacles in the way of the worship of the true God and, in the spirit of the Gelasian formula, left power to the state, while seeing in the Church the authority that came above all from the power of God's word.

Senator Symmachus, cited at the beginning of this section of the book, is perhaps in a certain sense rehabilitated: not in regard to his basically agnostic views on the pluralistic nature of truth about the mystery of God, but in regard to recognition of a religious pluralism that does not signify an absence of truth. This latter pluralism is, rather, the fruit of that religious freedom which the state should recognize in order not to exceed the limits of its competence and which the Church and any other religious society also should respect so as not to trample underfoot the legitimate freedom and dignity of the human person.

Above all, the Council helped the Church rediscover the spirit of its Lord Jesus and the apostles. They "strove to convert men to confess Christ as Lord, not however by applying coercion or with the use of techniques unworthy of the Gospel but, above all, by the power of the word of God."[38]

II. "Christian society" in the spirit of the Second Vatican Council and Josemaría Escrivá's spirit of love for freedom

A NEW WAY OF READING CATHOLIC TRADITION: FROM FREEDOM OF CONSCIENCES TO THE SPIRIT OF NONDISCRIMINATION

Undoubtedly, Josemaría Escrivá was a pioneer of the rediscovery of this spirit of profound respect for freedom marked

---

38. DH 11 (1072).

by rejection of all forms of coercion of consciences and of the use of violence to lead men to the truth. In one of his letters written for the formation of the members of Opus Dei, he insisted on "the Christian concern to eliminate any kind of intolerance, coercion, and violence in the dealing of men with one another. Also in apostolic activity—better: especially in apostolic activity—we don't want the slightest appearance of coercion to appear."[39] Since it is a matter of a foundational charism, this spirit was an essential part of Escrivá's preaching and activity from the beginning.

Naturally, this is formulated in the terminology of his time. The vast majority of his writings date from before the Council, when the way was not yet clear to speak of a "right to religious freedom," as the conciliar declaration *Dignitatis Humanae* was to do. Escrivá habitually used the formula introduced by Pope Pius XI[40] in reaction to the modern totalitarian movements; that is to say, he spoke of "freedom of consciences," an expression that summed up the perennial Catholic doctrine on the right of each person not to be constrained to act against his conscience, but said nothing about a right to follow one's conscience publicly and corporately. Yet, in using this expression, Escrivá, along with understanding its deepest and most essential meaning, brought out new and unsuspected consequences, as we shall see.

First, though, something needs clarifying. The term "freedom of consciences" expresses respect for the sanctuary of conscience, along with the fact that faith presupposes freedom, for only freely can one love the true God. In contrast, the "right to religious freedom" proposed by the Second Vatican Council is a juridical-political doctrine,[41] intimately connected with the previous concept but also distinct. It

39. Josemaría Escrivá, Letter of January 9, 1932, no. 66.

40. Encyclical *Non Abbiamo Bisogno*, of June 29, 1931, III, *Enchiridion delle Encicliche 5: Pio XI* (Bologna: Edizione Dehoniane, 1995): p. 815 (no. 780).

41. Cf. DH 2 (1045).

implies a particular conception of society and of politics, and it affirms the limitation of temporal power: the state is not competent in religious matters and must act in a manner that is neutral and impartial. In accord with Vatican II, however, the Church too must recognize its limits. Here, then, we have no less than the principle of *the essential secularity of the state.*

The message of Josemaría Escrivá does not operate at this last level, since it constitutes a spirituality or, better, a "spirit." One of its many features is the spirit of freedom and personal responsibility, which, nevertheless, transcends traditional formulas and opens the way to a much broader understanding. For example, in his homily on *Freedom, a Gift of God,* delivered in 1956, Escrivá speaks of "freedom of consciences," saying "it means that no one can licitly prevent a man from worshipping God. The legitimate hunger for truth must be respected. Man has a grave obligation to seek God, to know him and worship him, but no one on earth is permitted to impose on his neighbor the practice of a faith he lacks; just as no one can claim the right to harm those who have received the faith from God."[42] Escrivá wanted "the legitimate hunger for truth" to be respected, and he respected it even in those who did not share the Catholic faith with him.

Certainly, Escrivá understood this respect for the desire for truth in the framework of relations between persons, not in the juridical-political sense that provided the context for the teaching of the Second Vatican Council on the right to religious freedom. Precisely this spirit, preached ceaselessly by the founder of Opus Dei, explains his profound joy at the conciliar teaching, as reflected in something he said in an interview published in *Le Figaro* in 1966: "I have always defended the freedom of individual consciences. I do not understand violence. I do not consider it a proper way either to persuade or to win over. Error is overcome by prayer, by

---

42. *Friends of God,* no. 32.

by faith we know that the world's autonomy is relative and everything in this world has as its ultimate meaning the glory of God and the salvation of souls."[51] The question then arises: with this affirmation, haven't we returned to the Augustinian politics of St. Gregory, placing the earthly city at the service of the heavenly and the earthly powers at the service of the true religion? Aren't we looking at a new version of religious-political integralism?[52]

I want to repeat: the words of Josemaría Escrivá quoted above, written years before the Council, have as their context the preaching of a spirit that includes what Escrivá called "unity of life" as a basic imperative of the Christian life. This unity of life is not a political program, but a spiritual one. It reflects the words of St. Paul (1 Cor 10:31): "So, whether you eat or drink, or whatever you do, do all to the glory of God." Escrivá adds: "This doctrine of Holy Scripture, as you know, is to be found in the very nucleus of the spirit of Opus Dei. It leads you to do your work perfectly, to love God and mankind by putting love in the little things of everyday life, and discovering that divine something which is hidden in small details. . . . I assure you, my sons and daughters, that when a Christian carries out with love the most insignificant everyday action, that action overflows with the transcendence of God. . . . Heaven and earth seem to merge, my sons and daughters, on the horizon. But where they really meet is in your hearts, when you sanctify your everyday lives. . . . "[53]

What this means is that faith should shed light on a man's every step in this world, including his involvement in the earthly city. The Second Vatican Council, while emphasizing "the legitimate autonomy of temporal realities" in a celebrated passage, warned against the danger of using created

God's grace, and by study; never by force, always with charity. From the first moment this is the spirit we have lived. You can understand, then, how the Council's teaching on this subject could only make me happy."[43]

This is the context in which Escrivá interpreted the *compelle intrare* of Luke 14:23, which unfortunately became famous in the history of Catholic theology by the use made of it against the Donatists by St. Augustine: "This *compelle intrare* implies no violence, either physical or moral. Rather, it reflects the power of attraction of Christian example, which shows in its way of acting the power of God."[44] And, as if to rehabilitate the true Augustinian spirit, he added words of the holy Bishop of Hippo: "See how the Father attracts. He gives joy in his teaching, he imposes no necessity on men. That is how he attracts them toward himself."[45]

Given the panorama exhibited in the preceding pages, affirmations such as the following take on a very special significance: "In the Church and in civil society there are no second-class faithful or citizens. In apostolic as in temporal activities it is arbitrary and unjust to set limitations to the freedom of the sons and daughters of God, to the freedom of their consciences, or to their legitimate initiatives. Such limitations come about through abuses of authority, through ignorance, or through the error of those who permit themselves the abuse of discriminating in a way that can in no way be justified."[46]

In the mind of the founder of Opus Dei this vision was based on a profound theological perspective capable of surmounting the restrictive sectarian interpretations of the principle of nondiscrimination mentioned above. As we shall see below, Josemaría Escrivá preached a spirit of openness,

51. Josemaría Escrivá, Letter of January 9, 1959, no. 31.

52. Cf. also my reflections: "Neuevangelisierung und politische Kultur," *Schweizerische Kirchenzeitung* 62 (1994), no. 44, pp. 608–613; and no. 45, pp. 622–627.

53. Escrivá, Homily "Passionately Loving the World," in *Conversations*, no. 116.

43. *Conversations*, no. 44.

44. *Friends of God*, no. 37.

45. Ibid.

46. Josemaría Escrivá, Letter of March 11, 1940, no. 65.

because "we are friends of working peacefully with everyone precisely because we esteem, respect, and defend in all its great value the dignity and freedom that God has given to the rational creature, from the first moment of creation. And, even more, from the time that that same God did not hesitate to take on a human nature, and the Word became flesh and dwelt among men (Jn 1:14)."[47]

Just to read his writings is not sufficient fully to capture this spirit of Josemaría Escrivá. He was before all else a founder: a pastor, a father of his spiritual daughters and sons and of all who were linked to them by friendship or by collaboration in their various apostolic initiatives. He was also the initiator of numerous formative and social activities throughout the world that testify to this spirit of freedom and nondiscrimination. When in the fifties Escrivá asked the Holy See for authorization to accept non-Catholics and non-Christians as cooperators in Opus Dei, the first reaction was that he had come "a hundred years too soon." The founder repeated his request and finally obtained permission. Years later, Escrivá responded to a journalist by noting that, "from its foundation Opus Dei has never practiced discrimination of any kind. It works and lives with everyone because it sees in each person a soul that must be respected and loved. These are not mere words. Our Work is the first Catholic organization which, with the authorization of the Holy See, admits non-Catholics, whether Christian or not, as cooperators."[48]

Josemaría Escrivá's spirit of freedom and nondiscrimination is profoundly present in the Work he founded. His whole life was a witness to it.[49] Innumerable episodes illustrate his love for freedom and his openness of spirit. As an example, we recall that when receiving the visit of a non-Catholic, he

---

47. Ibid., no. 66.

48. *Conversations*, no. 44.

49. In this regard one need simply peruse any of the various biographies of Josemaría Escrivá.

explained that although he was convinced of the truth of Catholic religion, he would, with the help of God's grace, g his life to defend his visitor's freedom of conscience. T well-known Strathmore College in Nairobi, Kenya, a corp rate work of Opus Dei, was able to open its doors only af Escrivá decisively opposed the usual practice of the gover ment of that time and insisted that the institution must open to people of all colors and races without any discrimin tion. Thus, in the 1960s, Strathmore became the first racial mixed college in Black Africa. This insistence by the found of Opus Dei simply reflected his conviction that "we ar brothers, children of the same Father, God. So there is onl one race, the race of the children of God. There is only on color, the color of the children of God."[50]

TOWARD A CHRISTIAN SOCIETY: UNITY OF LIFE, FREEDOM, AND PERSONAL RESPONSIBILITY

This brief sketch would be incomplete if I failed to refer to another aspect in which this spirit of love for freedom and personal responsibility takes on the greatest importance: the public activity of faithful lay Christians and their work in organizing the earthly city and temporal structures according to the spirit of Christ. This is a broad theme allowing one again to consider the classic questions about the relationship between the temporal power and the spiritual authority of the Church, now represented in political society by the action of lay people who, in fidelity to the teachings of the Church, try to make human society conform to the spirit of Christ.

The founder of Opus Dei spoke decisively on this subject. In a letter he affirmed that "the message of Christ illuminates the whole life of mankind, its beginning and its end, not only in the narrow field of certain subjective practices of piety. And laicism is the negation of faith by deeds, whereas

---

50. *Christ Is Passing By*, no. 106.

things "without any reference to their Creator."[54] Thus it observed that "one of the gravest errors of our time is the dichotomy between the faith which many profess and the practice of their daily lives." This is the error of those who think "we may immerse ourselves in earthly activities as if these latter were utterly foreign to religion, and religion were nothing more than the fulfillment of acts of worship and the observance of a few moral obligations." There should be no such artificial "opposition between professional and social activity on the one hand and religious life on the other." The model for us is Christ, "who worked as a craftsman." Christians should devote themselves to "their earthly activity in such a way as to integrate human, domestic, professional, scientific, and technical enterprises with religious values, under whose supreme direction all things are ordered to the glory of God."[55]

This is the sense in which Fr. Escrivá spoke of "unity of life," and invited people to "know how to 'materialize' their spiritual life," so as not to give way to the temptation "of living a kind of double life. On one side, an interior life, a life of relation with God; and on the other, a separate and distinct professional, social, and family life, full of small earthly realities. No, my children! We cannot lead a double life. We cannot have a split personality if we want to be Christians. There is only one life, made of flesh and spirit. And it is that life which has to become, in both body and soul, holy and filled with God: we discover the invisible God in the most visible and material things."[56] For a Christian who lives and works *nel bel mezzo della strada*, as Escrivá frequently put it, smack in the middle of the world, which is good "because it has come forth from the hands of God," and which the ordinary Christian "loves passionately," there is naturally a clear sense

---

54. *Gaudium et Spes*, 36.
55. Ibid., 43.
56. "Passionately Loving the World," in *Conversations*, no. 114.

of having been called by God "to serve him *in and from* the ordinary, material, and secular activities of human life. He waits for us every day, in the laboratory, in the operating theatre, in the army barracks, in the university chair, in the factory, in the workshop, in the fields, in the home, and in all the immense panorama of work."[57]

It should be clear that this teaching cannot be understood as a political-religious program at the service of the ecclesiastical hierarchy and its specific pastoral mission. The founder of Opus Dei sees the laity—ordinary Christians, each one in the particular circumstances of his life—acting with a Christian, Catholic conscience, with full freedom and autonomy; and laying the world, not at the feet of the ecclesiastical hierarchy (to put it in those terms), but at the feet of Jesus: placing the Cross of Christ, his salvific love, at the summit of all human activities. The apostolate of the laity is for him not primarily a participation in the mission of the hierarchy. It is a participation, conferred directly through baptism, in the priestly mission of Jesus himself, though always carried out in close union with the legitimate pastors of the Church (the Roman Pontiff and the bishops in union with him) and in fidelity to its magisterium.

Therefore Escrivá does not conceive of the laity as a new secular arm of the Church. Its apostolate is not the "long arm" of the hierarchy.[58] Perhaps that was the vision that guided Pope Pius XI in promoting Catholic Action and the rebirth of a "Christian state" which, as a temporal power, would recognize the Catholic Church as the one voice of divine truth. That great Pontiff thought only of a purely pastoral mission permeated with a great spiritual strength, but in its juridical-political implications—and these are what concern us now—it

57. Ibid. For this aspect of "love for the world" one might see my work "Der selige Josemaría and die Liebe zur Welt," in César Ortiz, ed., *Josemaría Escrivá. Profile einer Gründergestalt.* (Cologne: Adamas Verlag, 2002): pp. 225–252.

58. Cf. *Conversations*, no. 21.

undoubtedly fell short of the more nuanced perspective of Vatican II. Already in his first encyclical, *Ubi Arcano*, Pius XI proposed a society under the guidance of a Church recognized by the state as the true and only teacher and guide of people. He also saw in the laity, organized in an effective way and guided by the hierarchy, an instrument to attain that end in all sectors of society. Only in this way, said the Pope, would the peace of Christ in the Kingdom of Christ, the *pax Christi in regno Christi*, be realized.[59]

Escrivá was, of course, not trying to set up his version of the apostolate of the laity in opposition to other forms. He loved diversity (freedom, that is), especially in ways of carrying out the one mission of the Church. He had a great appreciation for the work performed by Catholic Action at the service of the Church, so rich and varied in different times and places. But he remained faithful to the specific charism intended for Opus Dei: "Our mission is different. The others are working very well. But to work in that way, you already have these others. What God is asking of us is different; our way is lay, secular, a way of freedom and personal responsibility. *Spiritus ubi vult spirat* (Jn 3:8) (God's Spirit blows where he wishes). And he wants to inspire the Work of God with a special purpose and character, within the unity of the Church."[60]

All the same, point 301 of *The Way* echoes the theme of the pontificate of Pius XI that was mentioned above. This is characteristic of Escrivá's attitude of profound and filial union

---

59. Cf. *Enchiridion delle Encicliche* 5, 43f. (no. 37–39). Cf. also Pius XI, Encyclical *Quas Primas* on the institution of the Feast of Christ the King, *Enchiridion*, 158 ff., especially 183f. (no. 154f.).

60. *Letter* of August 5, 1953, no. 18, 2. I am not in a position to determine whether these words of Escrivá should be understood as opposition between the apostolate of Opus Dei and Catholic Action. Historians must shed light on that. But it does not seem farfetched to suppose that the author of the letter quoted had also thought about various forms of Catholic Action, at least—considering that the letter was written in 1953—of Catholic Action as understood by Pius XII, considerably more organized and centralized than it was in his predecessor's day (cf. Philippe Chenaux, *Pio XII. Diplomate et pasteur* [Paris: Éditions du Cerf, 2003]: p. 326ff.)

with the pope: "A secret, an open secret: these world crises are crises of saints. God wants a handful of men 'of his own' in every human activity. And then . . . '*pax Christi in regno Christi*—the peace of Christ in the kingdom of Christ'." Yet this does not have the "political" connotations of *Ubi Arcano*. The motto of the successor of St. Peter quickly acquired a different meaning in the mind of the founder of Opus Dei, faithful to his specific foundational charism. Not that Escrivá doubted the need for those Christians who are active in politics and in public affairs—as are all of the baptized—to seek to permeate all temporal structures with the spirit of Christ. "Nonsectarianism. Neutrality. Old myths that always try to seem new. Have you ever stopped to think how absurd it is to leave one's Catholicism aside on entering a university, a professional association, a cultural society, or Parliament, like a man leaving his hat at the door?"[61] But programmatic and organizational aspects are quite specifically left open. The theme of Pius XI acquires a more spiritual significance and at the same time opens up the perspective of an apostolic efficacy that permeates all areas of society. The laity are seen as acting with full freedom and with consequent personal responsibility, together with other men who in many cases do not share their faith. They are understood to be leaven, mixed into the mass of humanity, illuminating all human activities with the light of the faith and spreading the salt of good doctrine and the charity of Christ.

The idea of the reign of Christ in society is not a political program for Escrivá: "I do not approve of committed Christians in the world forming a political-religious movement. That would be madness, even if it were motivated by a desire to spread the spirit of Christ in all the activities of men. What we have to do is put God into the heart of every single person, no matter who he is. Let us try to speak then in such a way that every Christian is able to bear witness to the faith

---

61. *The Way*, no. 353.

he professes by example and word in his own circumstances, which are determined alike by his place in the Church and in civil life, as well as by ongoing events."[62]

Escrivá in this way was undoubtedly doing justice to the most profound aspirations of Pius XI, in whose pontificate Opus Dei had been born on October 2, 1928. Yet the difference in spirit is striking. Pius XI seemed still wedded to the traditional idea that it would be right for the Church to claim a special recognition from the public authorities of its spiritual mission because of its claim to be the only *true* Church—with all the juridical-political consequences such recognition implied. But the founder of Opus Dei seemed to perceive from the beginning that the principle of "freedom of consciences" so beloved by that pope, demanded something more. In his homily on the Feast of Christ the King, cited earlier, he emphasized that "if anyone saw Christ's kingdom in terms of a political program he would not have understood the supernatural purpose of the faith, and he would risk burdening consciences with weights which have nothing to do with Jesus, 'for his yoke is easy and his burden is light.' Let us really love all men; let us love Christ above all; and then we cannot avoid loving the rightful freedom of others, living in harmony with them."[63]

The Christian influence of Catholics on social structures and their role in bringing about a society permeated by the doctrine of Christ would thus be carried out in a spirit of love for "the rightful freedom of others" and "living in harmony with them." Even though Escrivá never theorized about the civil right to religious freedom—this was not his mission—he seems to have anticipated what would later be the spirit of the Second Vatican Council. It led the Church to recognize the secularity of the state at the juridical-political level: not a "laicist" state, but one lay and secular that gives no preference

---

62. *Christ Is Passing By*, no. 183.
63. Ibid., no. 184.

to any system of religious beliefs on the basis of its being the only true one, inasmuch as "truth can impose itself on the mind of man only in virtue of its own truth."[64]

THE SECULAR STATE, "CHRISTIAN SECULARITY," AND PLURALISM: THE RESPONSIBILITY OF THE ORDINARY CHRISTIAN BEFORE HISTORY

In the shelter of a lay state, understood in this way, a society and a political culture characterized by what I would call "Christian secularity" can grow. In this society the demands of truth and freedom are reconciled. The redemptive truth of Christ penetrates human society and all the structures of the world not by the coercive power of state power acting as the Church's "temporal arm," but by means of the unity of life of Christians who know how to live their ordinary lives with freedom and personal responsibility, as a participation in the priestly mission of Christ.

In the past, theology thought there was a necessary link between the permeation of human society by the Christian spirit on the one hand, and, on the other, public recognition of the truth of the Catholic religion and a privileged legal position for the Catholic Church—an established Catholic Church, that is to say. It resisted other views as signs of "indifferentism" and "laicism."

Since the Second Vatican Council, we know that this perspective was the result of a special historically conditioned interpretation that combined perennial truths with contingent and passing circumstances certainly not part of the deposit of faith. It is a perennial truth that the plenitude of revealed truth about God, man, and the world is only found in the Catholic Church, and that this Church is called to work so that the salvific spirit of Christ will permeate all earthly realities, especially human society. Catholics who wish to

---

64. DH 1 (1044).

remain faithful to their Christian vocation could never accept a "laicism" that would stand in the way of this truth and impede the efforts of the Church, its repository, visible, public, and organized as a juridical and pastoral organism, to infuse with the light of truth temporal realities, society, and the people who live in it.

The lay or secular state, on the contrary, knows that it is at the service of the common good. It extends impartial favor to private and communal practice of various religious beliefs, respecting their particular heritages and the cultural and religious circumstances of different people and nations, without any suggestion of sectarianism. Thus it is open to the salvific action of the Church of Christ. This is not an indifferentist vision, either of the various religions or of the Church or of society. The state would be indifferent only as an institution in the specifically juridical-political sense, as an essentially lay institution and not a secular branch of the Church. And it would open the way to Christian secularity: the vocation of the Christian, lived in human society with freedom and personal responsibility before men but also before a God who has revealed himself to men and redeemed us with his blood, communicating through his Church the truth and treasures of the new life in Christ.

In the course of the process of secularization the Church has undeniably lost much of its influence on society and over men and women. Some ask whether Christianity has a future.[65] From a historical and sociological point of view, it may very well be true that "the disappearance of the state norm of ecclesial membership" is the "most elemental and long-lasting cause of its decline," since "voluntariness is never as extensive as coercion."[66] Nevertheless, from the point of

---

65. Cf. Franz-Xavier Kaufmann, *Wie überlebt das Christentum?* (Freiburg i. B.: Herder, 2000).
66. Ibid., p. 118.

view of faith and in a theological perspective, one must insist that freedom is always, in the end, stronger than coercion; for faith opens men's hearts to the saving action of divine grace, which transforms, rebuilds, and produces the "fruits of the spirit," whereas coercion, although in the short run producing the appearance of religious penetration, leads to a simple external conformity and ends with dissolution, as history has so often demonstrated. In short, the Church today is called once more to believe in freedom: a freedom open to the transforming power of the gospel and of God's grace, but true freedom. In preparing the way to that "Christian secularity," Josemaría Escrivá's message was a leaven whose importance should not be underestimated.

We cannot go into great detail here on what Christian secularity specifically means at various levels. That may be a lesson for history to teach—a history made by Christians. History repeatedly opens up new horizons and overturns old formulae that turn out to be only seemingly exhaustive and definitive. History also bears the mark of freedom. At least that is how Josemaría Escrivá understood it: "God, in creating us, has run the risk and the adventure of our freedom. He has wanted a history that would be a true history, made up of authentic decisions and not a fiction nor a game. Each person has to experience his or her personal autonomy, with what this brings with it of hazard, of testing and, on occasion, of uncertainty."[67] It thus stands to reason that freedom should give rise to a true and legitimate pluralism in the course of history. For the consciences of believing Christians, pluralism will remain within the limits of the faith; but inevitably and legitimately, it will be much broader in a society characterized by diversity of religious beliefs and a plurality of cultural traditions, which defines itself by its recognition of the right of religious freedom.

---

67. Josemaría Escrivá, "The Riches of the Faith" (article in the newspaper *ABC*, Madrid, November 2, 1969, English translation in Scepter Booklet, *The Life of Faith*, 1974).

A society politically organized with secular institutions, constituted as an open society in this sense, and founded on religious freedom as taught by the Catholic Church, will always find confronting it the challenge of a pluralism that also includes elements perceived by a believing Catholic as erroneous and possibly dangerous to society's welfare and the temporal and eternal happiness of individuals.[68] This is the price of freedom.

A history made by Christians—ordinary Christians— would be the product of the efforts of those who, thanks to the light of the faith, know how to live their own freedom responsibly and seek to make that light a beacon, while always fully respecting the rights that arise from the freedom of their fellow citizens, including their right to be mistaken, to be in error, or to be indifferent.[69] At the same time, they try to collaborate loyally with all men in the broad space for the exercise of freedom that a secular and open political culture allows to all in searching for the common good. Respect for that liberty will ensure that the truth is never imposed by the force of coercion, due to a regrettable mixing of spiritual and temporal interests, but only imposes itself "in virtue of its own truth."[70] In this way, by means of a responsible exercise of their freedom and civil rights on the part of Christians, respect for liberty will also make it possible for society and all temporal realities to be shaped according to the spirit of Christ.

---

68. The importance of religious freedom and the corresponding neutrality of the state in this matter does not mean neutrality on the part of the secular or lay state in regard to certain substantial values of moral relevance. Some precisions on this point can be found in my article: "Lo Stato costituzionale democratico e il bene commune," in *Ripensare lo spazio politico: quale aristocrazia?* (edited by Emmanuele Morandi and Riccardo Panattoni) *Con-tratto—Rivista di filosofia tomista e contemporanea* VI (1997) (Padua: Il Poligrafo, 1998): pp. 57–122.

69. Cf. DH 2 (1046).

70. DH 1 (1044).

ORIGINS OF THE CHAPTERS
IN THIS VOLUME

1. Josemaría Escrivá and Love for the World
This chapter was originally published as a contribution to an anthology edited by César Ortiz in honor of the hundredth anniversary of the birth of St. Josemaría Escrivá and published in Cologne in 2002 under the title *Josemaría Escrivá: Profile einer Gründergestalt.*

2. Affirming the World and Christian Holiness
The chapter is taken from a talk given at a conference entitled "Christians in the Middle of the World" as part of the celebration of the hundredth anniversary of the birth of St. Josemaría at the Kongresshaus Zürich on June 15, 2002 and also at the 33rd Meeting of the *Internationale Priesterkreis* held from August 27–29, 2002 in the Maternushaus in Cologne under the title *"Der Wille Gottes: eure Heiligung"* (The Will of God: Your Sanctification). The text presented here has been substantially reworked and expanded.

3. The New Evangelization and Political Culture
This article appeared in 1994 in response to specific events then taking place and was originally published in the *Schweizerische Kirchezeitung* (SKZ) in two parts. For this reprinting it seemed best simply to eliminate the references to the particular problem at that time, which has since been solved. The remaining value of the

article and the reason for its republication is the fact that it deals with a central thesis of a well-known European critic of Opus Dei, Peter Hertel, and attempts to answer it fully and in a constructive manner.

4. Truth and Politics in a Christian Society

This is an expanded version of a paper given at the International Conference on *The Greatness of Ordinary Life* (Rome, January 8–11, 2002) for the hundredth anniversary of the birth of Josemaría Escrivá. It was published in Volume 5, 2 of the conference proceedings (*Figli di Dio nella Chiesa: Riflessioni sul messaggio di San Josemaría Escrivá. Aspetti culturali ed ecclesiastici*, edited by Fernando de Andrés, Rome: 2004, pp. 153–178), under the title *Il rapporto tra verità e politica nella società cristiana: Riflessioni storico—teologiche per la valutazione dell'amore della libertà nella predicazione di Josemaría Escrivá.*

BIBLIOGRAPHICAL NOTES

WRITINGS OF JOSEMARÍA ESCRIVÁ

The Way, New York: 2002. (This book first appeared in 1934 under the title, *Consideraciones Espirituales*. It was expanded and published in its present form under the title *Camino* [*The Way*] in Valencia in 1939.)

Furrow, London/New York: 1987.

The Forge, London/New York: 1988.

Holy Rosary, 3rd ed., London: 1978.

Christ is Passing By, Dublin/New York/Sydney: 1974 and 1985.

Friends of God, 2nd ed., London/New York: 1980.

The Way of the Cross, London/New York/Dublin: 1983.

In Love with the Church, London/New York: 1991.

Conversations with Msgr. Escrivá, Dublin: 1974. (This book contains interviews which the founder of Opus Dei granted to journalists of the international press, as well as a homily titled "Passionately Loving the World," which he gave at the University of Navarra.)

La Abadesa de Las Huelgas: Estudio teológico jurídico [*The Abbess of Las Huelgas: A theological and juridical study*] 2nd ed., Madrid: 1974. (This book has not yet been translated into English.)

SOME BOOKS ABOUT JOSEMARÍA ESCRIVÁ AND OPUS DEI

Berglar, Peter. *Opus Dei: Life and Work of its Founder Josemaría Escrivá*. Princeton: 1993.

Bernal, Salvador. *Msgr. Josemaría Escrivá de Balaguer: A Profile of the Founder of Opus Dei*. London/New York: 1977.

Casciaro, Pedro. *Dream and Your Dreams will Fall Short*. Princeton: 1998.

Coverdale, John F. *Uncommon Faith: the Early Years of Opus Dei*. New York: 2002.

Del Portillo, Álvaro. *Immersed in God* (an interview about Josemaría Escrivá with Cesare Cavalleri), Princeton: 1996.

Fuenmayor, Amadeo de; Gómez-Iglesias, Valentín; Illanes, José Luis. *The Canonical Path of Opus Dei: The History and Defense of a Charism*. Princeton/Chicago: 1994.

Gondrand, François. *At God's Pace: Josemaría Escrivá, Founder of Opus Dei*. New York/ London: 1988. (Original French edition: *Au pas de Dieu*, Paris: 1982.)

Le Tourneau, Dominique. *What is Opus Dei?* Cork/Dublin: 1989.

Messori, Vittorio. *Opus Dei: Leadership and Vision in Today's Catholic Church*. Washington: 1997.

Ortiz, César (ed.). *Josemaría Escrivá: Profile einer Gründergestalt*. Cologne: 2002.

Rodríguez, Pedro; Ocáriz, Fernando; Illanes, José Luis. *Opus Dei in the Church: An Ecclesiological Study of the Life and Apostolate of Opus Dei*. Dublin-Princeton: 1994.

Vázquez de Prada, Andrés. *The Founder of Opus Dei: The Life of Josemaría Escrivá*. Vol. 1: *The Early Years* (2001). Vol. 2: *God and Daring* (2003). Vol. 3: *The Divine Ways on Earth* (2005), Princeton and New York: 2001ff.

West, William. *Opus Dei: Exploding a Myth*. Sydney: 1987.

INDEX

A

Adam, 9
Adamas Verlag, viii
"Affirming the World and
    Christian Holiness"
    (Rhonheimer), viii
Africa, 111
agnosticism, 94, 95n13, 106
alter Christus ("another
    Christ"), ix, 59n51
Ambrose of Milan, St., 88
American colonies, 70
anticlericalism, 93
anti-Semitism, 46, 46n28
apostolate: Baptism and, viii;
    charity and, 86; Church and,
    5; clergy and, 6; coercion
    and, 107; freedom and, 107;
    hierarchy and, 14; holiness,
    universal call to and, 4; laity
    and, 6, 114; love for the
    world and, 3; Opus Dei and,
ix, x, 28–29, 115n60; ordi-
    nary life and, 5, 14, 20–22;
    religious and, 6, 14
Aristotle, 83
asceticism, 2, 16, 27n47, 37, 38,
    39, 41, 43, 46, 50, 58, 80
Augustine, St., ix, 14, 17, 65,
    89–90, 90–91, 92n10, 106,
    109, 112

B

Baptism, 19, 36n6, 49; aposto-
    late and, viii; holiness, uni-
    versal call to and, viii, 4, 5,
    34; rediscovery of, 5; voca-
    tion and, 5, 31–32, 53
beatitudes, 5
Bellarmine, St. Robert, 66
Benedictines, 51–52
Berglar, Peter, 26, 75
Bible. *See* Holy Scripture

Opus Dei: apostolate and, ix, x, 28–29, 115n60; charism of, ix–x; Church, hierarchical structure of and, viii; Escrivá, St. Josemaría and, 1, 28; formational program of, ix; founding of, 1, 117; freedom and, viii, 74–80, 110; holiness, universal call to and, 28, 32–33; Holy Scripture and, 15, 112; ideal of, 80; as an instrument of service, viii; integralism and, 74, 79–80; John Paul II, Pope and, x; nondiscrimination and, 110; as pastoral instrument, viii, 80; as Personal Prelature, viii, x, 28; prayer and, 14–15; purpose of, viii; Second Vatican Council and, ix; as secret organization, 79; vocation and, 29
ora et labora ("pray and work"), 51
ordinary Christians. *See* laity
ordinary life: apostolate and, 5, 14, 20–22; co-redeeming value of, 5; divine in, 10–11, 15; faith and, viii; freedom and, 60; greatness and value of, viii; holiness, universal call to and, 5, 31; Incarnation and, 8; love for the world and, 26–27, 47–52; rediscovery of, 5, 6, 33–38, 38–44, 44–52; Reformation and, 33–38, 38–44; sanctifi-

cation and, 13; sanctification of, 5, 27n47, 32; spirituality and, 6, 19, 52–53; unity of life and, 118; vocation and, 31, 32. *See also* Christian life; work
Ortiz, César, viii

P

paganism, 23, 88, 89
pagans, 19
Papal Revolution, 65
Paradise, 30
Passionately Loving the World (Escrivá), 1, 47
patience, 19
Paul, St., 13, 18, 19, 45, 57, 112
Paul VI, Pope, 58
peace, 64–65, 68
perfection, 52n36; Christian, 13–14n25, 27n47; Church and, 5; of love, 4; love for the world and, 30–31; personal, 50; salvation and, 50; Second Vatican Council and, 6; spirituality and, 12; state of, 6, 12, 13, 19; virtue and, 19, 50; work and, 18–19; world and, 30–31
Perkins, William, 37–38, 41n18
personal responsibility, 108; freedom and, 60, 84, 111–18; personal inadequacy and, x
Peter, St., 6, 35, 116
Pharisees, 78n47
Pietism, 38, 39
Pius IX, Pope, 94, 96, 98n18